Powerbase

Beginner

W0205112

Longman

David Evans

1 first words

HELLO **1** Write these words in your language.

2 Listen and repeat the words.

YES **3** Write these words under the correct pictures.

one dollar **yes** **coffee** **no**

____

____

____

____

IN A CAFÉ **4** Listen to a conversation in a café. Then fill the gaps with the words on these pages.

■ *Hello.*
○ __________
■ Yes?
○ Coffee.
■ Sorry?
○ Coffee!
■ __________ ?
○ Coffee! Coffee!
■ __________ ?
○ Oh! Coffee, __________ .
■ OK. Coffee.
○ __________ __________ .
■ One dollar.
○ One dollar? One dollar?
■ Oh, sorry. One dollar, __________ .
○ __________ .
■ Thank you.
○ Goodbye.
■ Thank you. __________

NOW YOU **5** Read the conversation.

GRAMMAR *to be* (1)

I, YOU

1 Fill the gaps with these words.

I'm **you're**

2 Listen and check. Then repeat.

3 Listen to this conversation. Practise it with your names.

Hello. I'm Maria.

And I'm John. Hello.

HE, SHE, IT

4 Listen and fill the gaps with these words. Then say the sentences.

He's **She's** **It's**

________ Wall Street.

________ Donald Trump.

________ Hillary Clinton.

5 Talk about other people in the class.

He's ...

She's ...

WE, THEY

6 Listen and fill the gaps with these words. Then say the sentences.

We're **They're**

7 Talk about yourselves and other people in the class.

We're … and … *They're … and …*

CHECK *to be*

I'm	(I am)
You're	(You are)
He's	(He is)
She's	(She is)
It's	(It is)
We're	(We are)
You're	(You are)
They're	(They are)

A QUIZ

8 How many of the people and things below do you know? Use *He's*, *She's*, *It's* and *They're* and say the names.

9 Listen and point at the people or things.

real world

Asking for things

CAN I HAVE ...?

1 Listen and repeat. Then say the question again.

Can I have a coffee, please?

SIX THINGS

2 Listen to six conversations. Number these things in the order that you hear them.

a ____________

b ____________

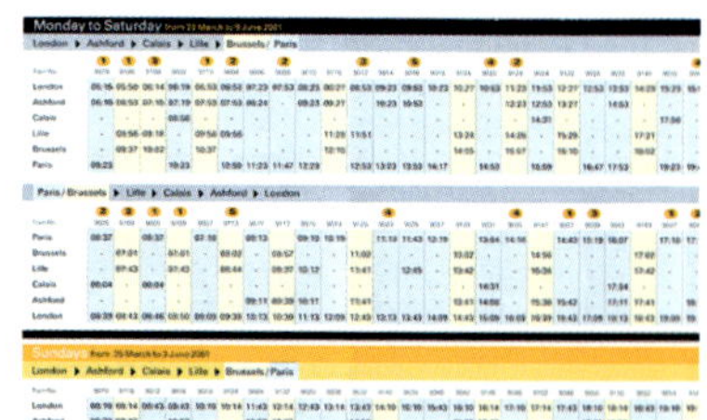

c ____________

d ____________

e ____________

f ____________

3 Listen again and write these words under the pictures.

the menu	the bill	a ticket	a map	a timetable	a coffee

4 Fill the gaps to make three sentences for a journey and three sentences for a restaurant.

A journey

1 Can I have *a timetable, please* ?
2 Can I have ____________ ?
3 ________ I have ________ , please?

A restaurant

1 ____________ the menu, please?
2 ________ I ____________ , please?
3 ______________________ ?

ORDERING A MEAL

5 Look at the menu. Which words do you know? Write them under the pictures.

1 ____________

2 ____________

London Heathrow to
Bangkok International

Menu

Tomato soup
Salad

Chicken and rice
Pasta

Fruit
Cheese

4 ____________

5 ____________

3 ____________

6 ____________

6 Listen to the conversation. What does the man choose from the menu?

NOW YOU

7 Choose some food from the menu. Then take turns to order your meal.

A Order your meal. Use *Can I have …, please?*
B Take the order and write it down.

2 surviving

ZERO TO 6

1 Listen and repeat. Then say the numbers again.

0	1	2	3	4	5	6
zero	one	two	three	four	five	six

2 Ask for these things. Use *Can I have …, please?*

3 menus   6 coffees   5 tickets   4 maps

3 Listen and check.

HOW MUCH IS IT?

4 Listen and repeat.

How much is it? **€2** *It's two euros.*

How much is it? **$6** *It's six dollars.*

5 Take turns. **A** Point at a picture. Ask *How much is it?* **B** Answer.

6 Listen and check.

PHONE NUMBERS

7 Take turns.

- **A** Read the phone numbers on page 74. **B** Write them down.
- **B** Read the phone numbers on page 77. **A** Write them down.

Read your numbers to check.

7 TO 12

8 Listen and repeat. Then say the numbers again.

7	8	9	10	11	12
seven	eight	nine	ten	eleven	twelve

WHAT TIME IS IT?

9 Listen and repeat.

What time is it? *It's nine o'clock.*

10 Look at the picture below. What time is it? Write and say the answers. Then listen and check.

1 It's _____ o'clock. *3* It's _____ o'clock. *5* It's _____ o'clock.
2 It's _____ o'clock. *4* It's _____ o'clock.

NOW YOU

11 Count backwards from 12 to 0. Take turns to say the numbers.

12 Take turns.

- **A** Read the numbers on page 74. **B** Write them down.
- **B** Read the numbers on page 77. **A** Write them down.

Read your numbers to check.

GRAMMAR *to be* (2)

ASKING QUESTIONS

1 Make questions from these sentences.

Example: You are Anna. ➡ Are you Anna?

1 He is Mike. ➡ _____ _____ _____?
2 You are OK. ➡ _____ _____ _____?
3 She is Leila. ➡ _____ _____ _____?
4 It is $5. ➡ _____ _____ _____?
5 They're sorry. ➡ _____ _____ _____?

2 Listen and check. Then listen and repeat.

CHECK Question form

Am I ... ?	Is he ... ?	Are we ... ?
Are you ... ?	Is she ... ?	Are you ... ?
	Is it ... ?	Are they ... ?

WHO* AND *HOW

3 Listen and repeat.

Who are you?

How are you?

4 Listen to two conversations. Then match these questions and answers.

Who are you?	Fine, thank you.
How are you?	I'm Yoshi.

5 Take turns to ask and answer the two questions above.

MORE QUESTIONS

6 Fill the gaps with the correct form of *to be*.

1 How much ___ it?
2 Who ___ they?
3 How ___ he?
4 ___ you Stan?
5 What time ___ it?
6 ___ she Maria?

7 Listen and check.

SHORT ANSWERS

8 Listen and repeat.

Are you Anna? → Yes, I am. / No, I'm not.

Is it €10? → Yes, it is. / No, it isn't.

CHECK Short answers

+	−
Yes, he is.	No, he isn't.
Yes, they are.	No, they aren't.

For more, go to page 83.

9 Take turns to ask and answer questions about each other. Then talk about other people in the class.

Are you … ? *Is he … ?* *Is she … ?*

WHO ARE THEY?

10 Fill the gaps. Ask questions and use short answers. Then listen and check.

1 Is he Ronald Reagan?

No, he isn't. He's John F. Kennedy.

2 ___ ___ Gwyneth Paltrow?

____

3 ___ ___ Anna Kournikova?

____

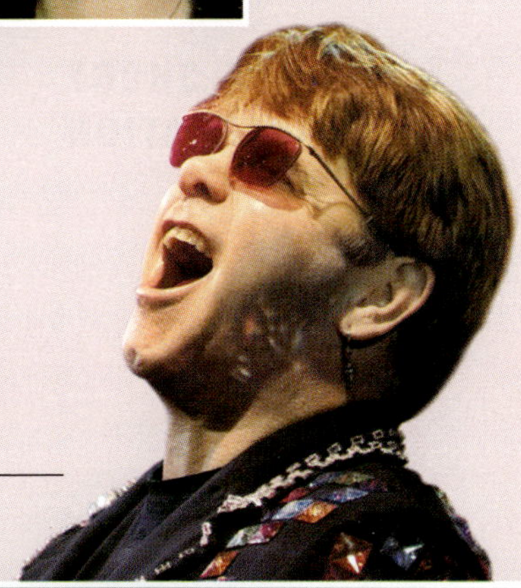

4 ___ ___ George Michael?

____

5 ___ ___ the Eiffel Tower?

____

6 ___ ___ The Spice Girls?

____

real world *Checking*

I DON'T UNDERSTAND

1 Listen and tick (✓) the phrases you hear. Then write them in your language.

2 Listen and repeat the phrases.

CHECKING NUMBERS

3 **A** Read the numbers on page 74. **B** Write them down.
B Read the numbers on page 77. **A** Write them down.
Use the phrases above to check.

Three. *Can you say that again, please?* *Yes. Three.*

A SHORT CONVERSATION

4 Listen and fill the gaps.

- ■ What time ______ ______ ?
- ○ Can you ______ ______ again, please?
- ■ What ______ is it?
- ○ Can you ______ more slowly, please?
- ■ ______ – time – is – it?
- ○ Oh! Five ______ .
- ■ Sorry?
- ○ ______ o'clock.
- ■ Thank you.

5 Listen again and check. Then read the conversation.

COMMUNICATION PROBLEMS

6 Look at this conversation. Can you fill the gaps?

■ Hello. Can I ______ a map, ______ ?
○ I'm sorry. I don't ______ .
■ A map. ______ ______ have ______ ______ , please?
○ Oh, a map. Yes. Of course.
■ How much ______ ______ ?
○ I'm sorry. ______ ______ say that again?
■ ______ ______ ______ ______ ?
○ It's $12.10, ______ .
■ Can you speak ______ ______ , please?
○ I'm sorry. $12.10, please.
■ $12.10. Thank you.
○ ______ ______ . Goodbye.

7 Listen and check. Then read the conversation.

NOW YOU

8 Role play this situation in a café. Use some of the questions in the box and others that you know.

A Ask for a coffee and ask *How much is it?* **B** Turn to page 77.

Can I have ...? **Can you say that again, please?** **Can you speak more slowly, please?** **How much is it?**

9 **B** You are in a station in New York. Ask for a ticket to Central Avenue and ask *How much is it?* **A** Turn to page 74.

10 Role play a situation at a party. Ask and answer questions in the box and others that you know.

Who are you? **How are you?** **Who is he?** **Who is she?** **What time is it?**

review 1

VOCABULARY
Crossword

1 Complete this crossword with words from Units 1 and 2. (You can find wordlists on pages 100–101.)

Across ▶

1 How _ _ _ _ is it?

3 

5 Four + three = _ _ _ _ _

6 ~~No.~~

7 

9 It's nine o'_ _ _ _ _ _.

11 Ten, nine, _ _ _ _ _

13 

14 How are you? _ _ _ _, thank you.

15 Nine, ten, _ _ _ _ _ _

Down ▼

2 Can I _ _ _ _ the bill, please?

4 A coffee, _ _ _ _ _ _ _.

5 

8 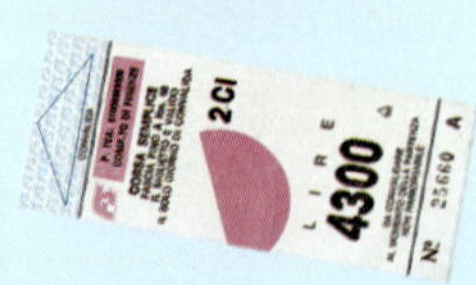

9 

10 Can you say it _ _ _ _ _, please?

12 We, you, _ _ _ _

GRAMMAR CHECK
to be

2 Fill the gaps.

I am = I'm	He is = He____	We ____ = We're
You ____ = You're	She ____ = She's	You ____ = You____
	It is = It____	They ____ = They____

3 Fill the gaps in these questions and answers.

1 What time is it ?	It's twelve o'clock.
2 Are you Tony?	No, ____ ____ . I'm Jacques.
3 Who ____ ____ ?	She's Georgina.
4 Is it five o'clock?	No, ____ ____ . It's four o'clock.
5 How much ____ ____ ?	They're $5.

PRONUNCIATION
Stress

4 Listen and notice the stress in these words. Then listen again and repeat.

coffee ticket again tomato eleven understand

FOCUS ON ...
Greetings

5 Which phrases mean *Hello* and which phrases mean *Goodbye*? Listen and then write them in the correct group.

See you. Good morning. Good night.
Hi. Good evening. Good afternoon.

hello

goodbye

6 Listen and check. Then repeat.

7 When do you say these phrases? Match them to the times.

Good morning. Good afternoon. Good evening. Good night.

3 people

WHAT'S YOUR NAME?

1 Listen and repeat.

name **job** **company** **country**

2 Listen and then write these words in the correct places.

Boris Netzer **Germany**
businessman **City Consulting**

Name	*Boris Netzer*
Job	
Company	
Country	

3 Listen and then take turns to ask and answer.

What's your name? *My name's ...*

WHAT'S YOUR JOB?

4 Match these jobs to the pictures.

a businessman **a student**
a businesswoman **a teacher**

5 Listen and check. Then repeat.

6 Take turns to ask about jobs. Use the words above and short answers.

Are you a businessman?
No, I'm not.
Are you a student?
Yes, I am.

What's your job?

I'm a ...

WHERE ARE YOU FROM?

7 These are the English names of the G8 countries. Listen and repeat.

Italy	France	the UK	Japan
Germany	Russia	the USA	Canada

8 Match the numbers on the map to the countries above.

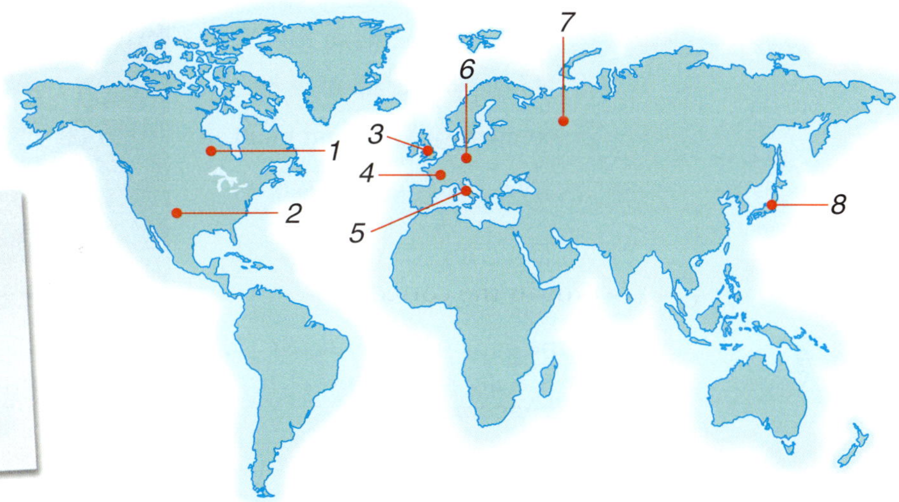

Where are you from?

I'm from ...

PERSONAL QUESTIONS

9 Listen and repeat.

What's your name? **What's your job?**
What's the name of your company? **Where are you from?**

10 Listen and then fill the gaps in these conversations.

On the phone

■ Hello. PP.com.
○ Oh, hello. Patrick Partridge, _____ .
■ Yes, of course. What's your _____ ?
○ _____ name's Jane Fong.
■ What's the name of your _____ ?
○ _____ City Consulting.
■ Just a moment, please.

At a party

■ I'm sorry. Are you from City Consulting?
○ No, _____ _____ .
■ Oh. What's the _____ of your company?
○ I'm not from a company. I'm _____ student.
■ _____ are you from?
○ I'm _____ the USA.
■ The USA? Really?

NOW YOU

11 Take turns to ask and answer questions about these things.

name? **job?** **company?** **country?**

GRAMMAR Possessive adjectives

GEORGE SOROS

1 Listen and read.

His name's George Soros. He's a businessman from Hungary. The name of his company is Quantum Fund.

2 Fill the gaps with *he, his* or *its.*

What's _his_ name?	_____ name's George Soros.
What's _____ job?	_____ 's a businessman.
Where's _____ from?	_____ 's from Hungary.
What's the name of _____ company?	_____ name is Quantum Fund.

3 Listen and check. Then take turns to read your questions and answers.

CARLY FIORINA

4 Listen and then fill the gaps with *she, her* or *its.*

What's _her_ name?	_____ name's Carly Fiorina.
What's _____ job?	_____ 's a businesswoman.
Where's _____ from?	_____ 's from the USA.
What's the name of _____ company?	_____ name's Hewlett-Packard.

5 Take turns to read your questions and answers.

6 Talk about other people in the class.

What's his/her name?

What's his/her job?

What's the name of his/her company?

CHECK Possessive adjectives

I	**my**	he	**his**	we	**our**
you	**your**	she	**her**	you	**your**
		it	**its**	they	**their**

For more, go to page 81.

PLURALS

7 Write these words on the correct line.

person **company** **jobs** **names** **name** **job**
women **people** **men** **companies** **woman** **man**

SINGULAR	*person*					
PLURAL	*people*					

8 Listen and check. Then repeat.

DAVE AND JERRY

9 Fill the gaps in the text with these words.

names **our** **company** **It's** **businessmen**

Hello! Our *names* **are Dave Filo and Jerry Yang. We're ______ and we're from California in the USA. The name of ______ company is Yahoo! ______ an Internet ______.**

YAHOO!

10 Write questions.

1 *What are their names*? Their names are Dave Filo and Jerry Yang.
2 ______? They're businessmen.
3 ______? They're from California.
4 ______? Its name is Yahoo!

11 Listen and check. Then take turns to ask and answer the questions.

NOW YOU

12 **A** Ask questions about picture 1. **B** Turn to page 77 and answer.
B Ask questions about picture 2. **A** Turn to page 74 and answer.

1

2

real world *Telephoning*

PHONE PHRASES

1 Listen and repeat.

A COMPANY CALL

2 Listen and then fill the gaps with these sentences.

Hello. City Consulting. **What's the name of your company?**
Can you say that again, please? **Just a moment, please.**
Can I speak to Tom Rogers, please?

■ *Hello. City Consulting.*
○ Hello. It's Luisa Briggs here. ____________________
■ Tom Rogers? Of course. ____________________
○ I'm from PA.com.
■ ____________________
○ I'm from PA.com.
■ Thank you. ____________________

3 Role play this phone conversation. Then swap roles.

A Call B, say your name and ask to speak to Maria.
B Answer the phone, ask A to say his/her name again and then ask for the name of A's company.

WHERE AND HOW

4 Match the questions and answers. Then take turns to ask and answer the questions.

How are you?	I'm from the USA.
Where are you?	Fine, thank you.
Where are you from?	I'm in a classroom.

CALLING A TAXI

5 Fill the gaps in the phone conversation with these sentences.

Hello. A1 Taxis. **Can you speak more slowly, please?**
Where are you? **At the airport.** **What's your name?**

■ *Hello. A1 Taxis.*
○ Oh, hello.
■ Just a moment, please. Yes. Hello.
○ Hello. Can I have a taxi, please?
■ Sure. ______________
○ David Norman.
■ David Norman. ______________
○ I'm at the airport.
■ ______________
○ Yes. I'm – at – the – airport.
■ ______________ Fine. Five minutes, OK?
○ Yes. Thank you. Goodbye.

6 Listen and check.

7 Role play this phone conversation. Then swap roles.

A You are at the Ritz Hotel. Phone and ask for a taxi.
B Answer the phone, ask for A's name and ask *Where are you?*

NOW YOU

8 Role play this situation. Then swap roles.

A You want some information about B. Phone him/her and ask the questions in the box and others that you know.
B Get ready to answer the questions.

Where are you? **What's the name of your company?** **How are you?**
Where are you from? **What's your job?** **Can you say that again, please?**

4 arrangements

SIX VERBS

1 Listen and repeat.

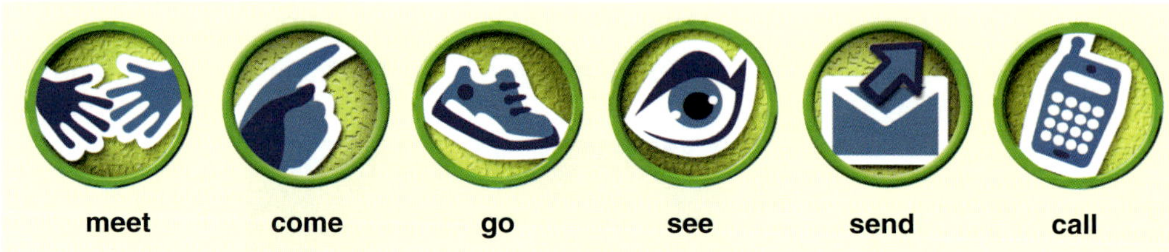

2 Choose the right verbs in this note.

Friday

COSMO HOTEL

Doris,

Can we see / meet at three o'clock on Monday? You can come / send to my hotel or I can see / go to your office. Please call / go on 010 4456 1123 or go / send an e-mail. See / Come you on Monday!

Bruce

3 Listen and check.

DAYS OF THE WEEK

4 Listen and repeat.

Monday	Thursday
Tuesday	Friday
Wednesday	Saturday
	Sunday

5 Take turns to ask and answer questions using *before* (↶) and *after* (↷).

Which day is before Wednesday? — *Tuesday.*

Which day is after Thursday? — *Friday.*

MEETING PLACES

6 Match the two parts of the sentences. (Use a dictionary to help you.)

You live in	an office.
You stay in	an apartment.
You work in	a restaurant.
You eat in	a shop.
You shop in	a hotel.

CHECK Articles

a + consonant
– a shop

an + vowel
– an office

For more, go to page 80.

7 Listen and check. Then repeat.

PREPOSITIONS

8 Listen and repeat.

come to	Can you come to my apartment?
go to	Can we go to your office?
meet at	Can we meet at your shop?
at	Can we meet at 5 o'clock?
on	Can we meet on Thursday?

9 Fill the gaps with *to*, *at* or *on*.

1 Can I come __*to*__ your hotel __*at*__ ten o'clock __*on*__ Thursday?

2 Can we go _____ the restaurant _____ Monday?

3 Can we meet _____ your shop _____ four o'clock _____ Friday?

4 Can you come _____ my office _____ two o'clock?

NOW YOU

10 Make questions.

1 we go / your shop / Tuesday
Can we go to your shop on Tuesday?

2 we meet / your office / 3 o'clock
____

3 you come / my hotel / Wednesday
____

4 we go / the restaurant / 6 o'clock
____

5 I come / your apartment / Thursday
____

GRAMMAR *can* and *can't*

CAN QUESTIONS

1 Match the two parts of these questions.

Can I speak	that again?
Can they come	to Maria, please?
Can you say	to my office on Monday?
Can you speak	a coffee, please?
Can I have	at the restaurant?
Can we meet	more slowly, please?

CHECK *can*

+ I can come.
– I can't come.
? Can I come?

For more, go to page 80.

2 Listen and check. Then repeat.

CAN AND *CAN'T*

3 Complete the sentences with these phrases. Then listen and check.

you can't call people, but you can send e-mails
you can call people and you can send e-mails
you can call people, but you can't send e-mails

With this phone _____ .

With this mobile phone _____ .

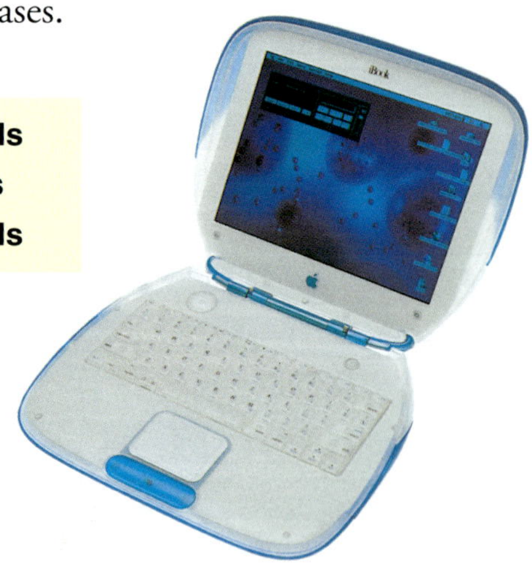

With this computer _____ .

4 Fill the gaps in these sentences.

1 Can you come to my office on Monday?
No, I'm sorry, *I can't come* on Monday, but I can come on Tuesday.

2 Can we meet on Thursday?
No, I'm sorry, _____ _____ _____ on Thursday, but we can meet on Friday.

3 Can I call on Friday?
No, I'm sorry, you can't call on Friday, but _____ _____ _____ on Saturday.

4 _____ _____ _____ to Frank, please?
No, I'm sorry, you can't speak to Frank, but _____ _____ _____ to Anna.

SHORT ANSWERS

5 Tick (✓) the correct answer.

1 Can you come to the restaurant on Thursday?
a Yes, I am. *b* Yes, I can. ✓
2 Are you a businessman?
a Yes, I am. *b* Yes, I can.
3 Can he send e-mails from his mobile phone?
a No, he isn't. *b* No, he can't.
4 Is she a teacher?
a No, she isn't. *b* No, she can't.

CHECK Short answers

Can she call on Tuesday?
No, she can't.

Is she a businesswoman?
Yes, she is.

For more, go to page 83.

A PHONE ARRANGEMENT

6 Listen and then fill the gaps with these phrases.

Can I **It's** **she can't** **Can she** **I can**
you can't **she can** **I'm** **are you** **Can you**

■ Hello. *Can I* speak to Maggie Khan, please?
○ No, I'm sorry, ______ ______ . She's in a meeting. Can I help you? ______ Maggie's secretary.
■ Oh, yes. ______ Nasser Hutchins here.
○ Nasser Hutchins. Which company ______ ______ from?
■ I'm from the BB Bank.
○ I'm sorry. ______ ______ say that again?
■ Sorry, yes. I'm from the BB Bank. Can Maggie meet me in London on Tuesday?
○ No, I'm sorry, ______ ______ . She's in New York on Tuesday.
■ Oh. ______ ______ meet me on Monday?
○ Monday? Yes, ______ ______ . Can you come to her office at one o'clock?
■ Yes, ______ ______ . One o'clock. Thank you.
○ Thank you. Goodbye.

7 Listen again and check. Then read the conversation.

NOW YOU

8 Arrange to go to a restaurant for lunch (around 12 o'clock – 3 o'clock). Take turns to ask and answer questions.

A Your diary is on page 74. **B** Your diary is on page 77.

Can you go to the restaurant on Friday?

No, I can't.

real world *E-mail*

E-MAIL WORDS

1 Which words come at the start of an e-mail and which words come at the end? Write them in the correct group.

Hi **Best wishes** **Regards** **Dear** **PS**

at the start of an e-mail	at the end of an e-mail
Hi	

2 Look at the two e-mails below and check.

AN E-MAIL ARRANGEMENT

3 Read the two e-mails and answer these questions.

1 When is Jill's plane?
2 Can Clara meet Jill on Wednesday?
3 When can she meet Jill?
4 How can they speak when Clara isn't in the office?

4 Listen and check.

From: Jill Nagano
To: Clara Hearst
Subject: Wednesday

Dear Clara,
My plane is at 12 o'clock on Wednesday.
Can we meet at your office at 4 o'clock?
Best wishes,
Jill

From: Clara Hearst
To: Jill Nagano
Subject: The meeting

Hi Jill,
Thank you for the e-mail. I'm sorry, but I can't meet you on Wednesday.
How about Thursday?
Regards,
Clara
PS When I'm not in the office, you can call my mobile phone: 0789 435 212.

AN E-MAIL JUMBLE

5 Put these sentences in the right order to make an e-mail.

Dear Kerry,	1
How about Thursday?	
Thank you for the e-mail.	
Please send an e-mail or call my mobile phone.	
Regards, Tom	
I'm sorry, I can't go to your shop on Friday.	

NOW YOU

6 You can't meet on Wednesday, but you can meet on Thursday. Write a reply to this e-mail.

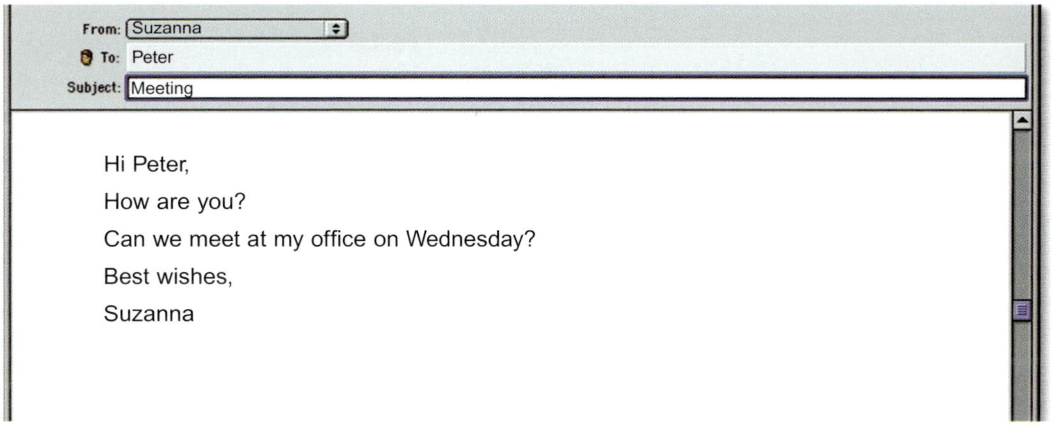
From: Suzanna
To: Peter
Subject: Meeting

Hi Peter,
How are you?
Can we meet at my office on Wednesday?
Best wishes,
Suzanna

7 Write an e-mail to come *before* this one.

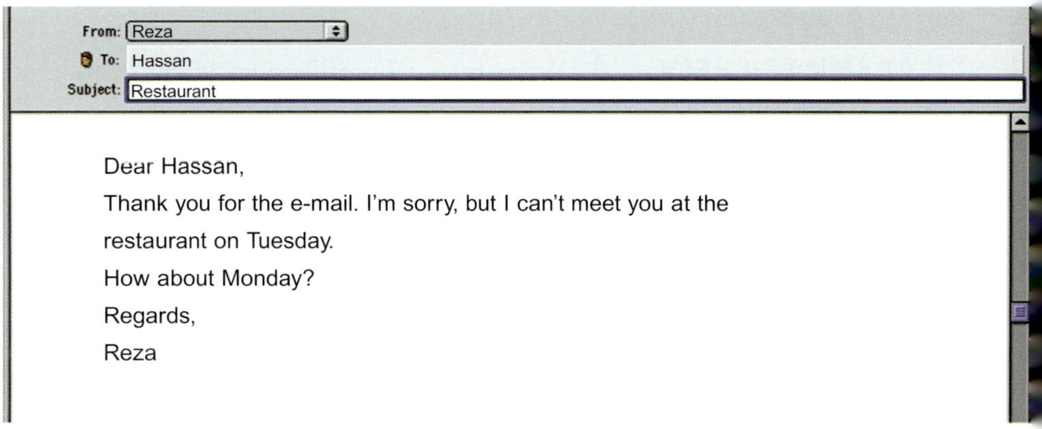
From: Reza
To: Hassan
Subject: Restaurant

Dear Hassan,
Thank you for the e-mail. I'm sorry, but I can't meet you at the restaurant on Tuesday.
How about Monday?
Regards,
Reza

8 Compare your e-mails.

9 Write an e-mail to your partner to make an arrangement. Reply to your partner's e-mail.

review 2

VOCABULARY
Verbs and nouns

1 Which words are verbs? Which words are nouns? Write them in the correct group. (Use a dictionary to help you.)

person	**go**	**woman**	**send**	**have**
office	**live**	**eat**	**company**	**hotel**

verbs

nouns

2 What are the plurals of the nouns in your list?

3 Look back at Units 3 and 4. Find five more verbs which are useful for you. Then compare.

GRAMMAR CHECK
Possessive adjectives and *can*

4 Write possessive adjectives in the gaps.

I *my*	he ____	we ____
you ____	she ____	you ____
	it ____	they ____

5 Put these sentences in the right order.

1 on Thursday / go to / she can't / the meeting
She can't go to the meeting on Thursday.

2 please / a taxi / have / can I ______

3 my office / come to / can you / on Friday ______

4 from his hotel / send e-mails / he can't ______

5 meet / on Wednesday / we can / at your shop ______

6 our apartment / come to / on Monday / can they ______

PRONUNCIATION
Sound and spelling

6 Listen to these words. Which letters can't you hear? Put a cross (✗) through them.

eight two where
what who Wednesday

7 Listen and repeat. Notice the difference.

her here

8 Take turns to say these words. Then listen and check.

mobile phone name plane before
office come rice nine have

FOCUS ON …
Spelling

9 Listen and repeat the letters of the alphabet. After each group of letters, pause and take turns to ask and answer the questions.

A B C D
Can you spell *bad*?
Can you spell *cab*?

E F G H
Can you spell *face*?
Can you spell *hedge*?

I J K L
Can you spell *Jack*?
Can you spell *bill*?

M N O P
Can you spell *phone*?
Can you spell *mail*?

Q R S T U
Can you spell *quiet*?
Can you spell *trust*?
Can you spell *restaurant*?

V W X Y Z
Can you spell *wave*?
Can you spell *why*?
Can you spell *X-ray*?
Can you spell *zero*?

10 Take turns to ask and answer these questions.

Can you spell your name?
Can you spell the name of your country?
Can you spell the name of your company?

11 Take turns to ask each other to spell five words from Units 3 and 4.

5 travel

TRAINS AND PLANES

1 Listen and repeat.

station	check-in	boarding gate
airport	ticket office	platform

2 Which words go with trains and which words go with planes? (Use a dictionary to help you.)

train	plane
station	

13 TO 29

3 Listen and repeat. Then say the numbers again.

13	14	15	16	17	18	19
thirteen	fourteen	fifteen	sixteen	seventeen	eighteen	nineteen
20	21	22	23 …	29		
twenty	twenty-one	twenty-two	twenty-three …	twenty-nine		

4 Look at this information. Ask and answer questions.

Which is the platform for Moscow?

It's platform fifteen.

MOSCOW		ISTANBUL	
Platform	15	Platform	14
PARIS		ATHENS	
Platform	19	Platform	13
BERLIN		MADRID	
Platform	17	Platform	22

30 TO 100

5 Listen and repeat. Then say the numbers again.

30	40	50	60	70	80	90	100
thirty	forty	fifty	sixty	seventy	eighty	ninety	a hundred

6 Match the words and the numbers.

twenty-one	15:45
two thirty	19
forty-four	21
fifteen forty-five	136
twenty-two fifty	44
a hundred and thirty-six	2:30
nineteen	22:50

7 **A** Read the numbers and times on page 75.
B Write them down, then read them to check.

B Read the numbers and times on page 78.
A Write them down, then read them to check.

ANNOUNCEMENTS

8 Listen and fill the gaps.

1

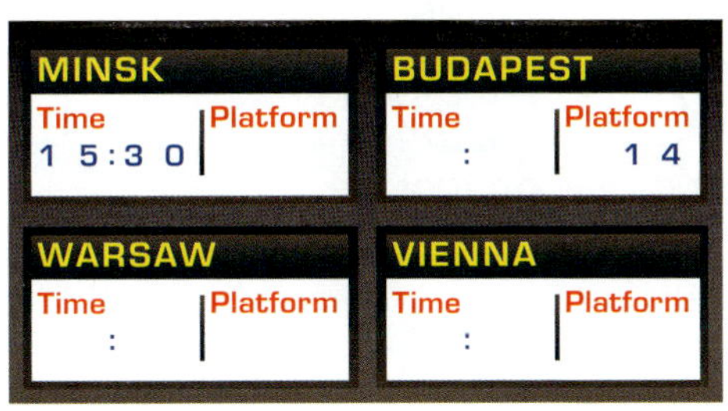

2

9 Ask and answer questions about the two boards.

What time is the train to Minsk?

It's at 15:30.

Which is the gate for Atlanta?

It's gate 42.

GRAMMAR Present simple (1)

A BRAZILIAN BUSINESSWOMAN

1 Listen and read. Then answer the questions.

My name's Sasha Amado. I'm a businesswoman from Brazil. I live in Santos and I work in São Paulo. I have a VW and I go to work by car.

1 What's her name? *Sasha Amado*
2 What's her job? ______
3 Where's her apartment? ______
4 Where's her office? ______
5 How does she go to work? ______

2 Write sentences about yourself. Use the phrases in the box to help you.

I live in ...
I work in ...
I go to work ...

CHECK Positive

I live	She lives
I work	She works
I go	She goes
I have	She has

For more, go to page 82.

ASKING QUESTIONS

3 Match the sentences with the same meaning.

Where's your apartment?	What do you do?
Where's your office?	Where do you live?
What's your job?	Where do you work?

4 Put the verb in brackets ( ) into the correct form to make a question.

How (you go) to work? ______

CHECK Question form

+	?
You live	Do you live?
You work	Do you work?

For more, go to page 82.

5 Take turns to ask and answer questions.

Where / live? Where / work?
What / do? How / go to work?

A FRENCH BUSINESSMAN

6 Fill the gaps with these words.

has **lives** **is** **goes**

Claude Ozawa ______ a businessman from France. He ______ in Versailles and he works in Paris. He ______ a Renault and he drives to work.

His company also has offices in London and New York. Claude ______ to London by train, but, of course, he flies to New York.

7 Answer these questions about Claude Ozawa.

1 How does he go to work in Paris? ______________

2 How many offices does his company have? ______________

3 How does he go to New York? ______________

8 Write more questions about Claude Ozawa. Put the verbs in brackets ( ) into the correct form.

1 What (he do)? ______________

2 Where (he live)? ______________

3 What car (he have)? ______________

4 Where (he work)? ______________

5 How (he go) to London? ______________

9 Take turns to ask and answer the questions.

NOW YOU

10 Take turns.

A Read about the man on page 75.
B Ask these questions about him.

What / name? What / do?
Where / live? Where / work?
How / go to work?

B Read about the woman on page 78.
A Ask the same questions about her.

CHECK Question form

+	?
He has	**Does** he have?
He does	**Does** he do?

For more, go to page 82.

real world

Travel information

INFORMATION, PLEASE

1 Listen and repeat.

Can I have some information about the plane to Seoul, please?
What time does it leave?
What time does it arrive?

2 A woman is asking about a plane to Seoul. Listen and answer these questions.

1 What time does the plane leave? _____

2 What time does it arrive? _____

AN E-MAIL ENQUIRY

3 This is an e-mail from a businesswoman to her travel agent. What information does she want?

From: Rita Monte
To: James Corelli, Rosa Travel
Subject: Train to Madrid

Dear James,
Can I have some information about the train from Paris to Madrid on Saturday morning? Which station in Paris does it leave from? What time does it leave? And what time does it arrive in Madrid?
Thank you for your help.
Best wishes,
Rita Monte

4 This is the reply to the e-mail. Put it in the right order.

It leaves at 9:15 and arrives at 22:30.
Regards,
Thank you for your e-mail.
James Corelli (Business travel co-ordinator)
Dear Ms Monte,
The train to Madrid on Saturday morning goes from Gare d'Austerlitz.

INFORMATION ROLES

5 Role play these situations.

- **A** Call B and ask for information about the train to Paris on Tuesday. Find out what time it arrives and what time it leaves.
  B Look at the information on page 78 and answer A's questions.
- **B** Call A and ask for information about the plane to Tokyo on Wednesday. Find out what time it arrives and what time it leaves.
  A Look at the information on page 75 and answer B's questions.

STATIONS AND AIRPORTS

6 Listen to two conversations and fill the gaps.

1)

Plane to: Bangkok
Leaves at:
Arrives at:
Boarding gate:

2)

Train to: Turin
How much:
Leaves at:
Arrives at:
Platform:

NOW YOU

7 Role play these situations.

- **A** You want a train ticket to Berlin. At the station ticket office, ask about:
  ticket to Berlin? how much? time / leave? time / arrive? platform?
  B Turn to page 78 and answer.
- **B** You want to fly to Mexico City. At the airport check-in, ask about:
  time / leave? time / arrive? boarding gate?
  A Turn to page 75 and answer.

6 work

WHAT DO THEY DO?

1 Listen and repeat.

1 a factory worker ________

2 a boss ________ a secretary ________ *3* a salesperson ________ a customer ________

2 Listen to five people. Then write these verbs next to the right person.

sells **helps** **buys** **manages** **makes**

> **What do you do?**
>
> I ...

3 Which verbs in the box go before 'people' and which verbs go before 'things'?

________ + **people** ________ + **things**

4 Take turns. Point at the pictures above and ask *What does he/she do?* Answer with the name of the job and then say what he/she does.

What does he do? *He's a salesperson. He sells things.*

WHO DO THEY WORK FOR?

5 Complete these sentences. Then listen and check.

Who *does he work for?*

He works for BP.

Who ____ ____ work for?

____ ____ ____ Compaq.

____ ____ they ____ ____ ?

____ ____ ____ Vodafone.

6 Take turns to ask and answer questions.

Who do you work for?

I work for …

WHAT KIND OF COMPANY IS IT?

7 Listen and repeat.

a manufacturing company **a supermarket** **a charity**

8 Complete the sentences with these phrases.

a supermarket **sells** **a charity** **does it do**
kind of **helps** **makes** **a manufacturing company**

TESCO

TOYOTA

Save the Children

1. What kind of company is Tesco? It's *a supermarket* .
   What does it do? It *sells* food.
2. What ________ company is Toyota? It's ________ .
   What does it do? It ________ cars.
3. What kind of company is Save the Children? It's ________ .
   What ________ ? It ________ children.

NOW YOU

9 Look at these questions and think about your answers. (Use a dictionary to help you.) Then take turns to ask and answer the questions.

What do you do? **What kind of company is it?** **Who do you work for?** **What does it do?**

GRAMMAR Present simple (2)

POSITIVE AND NEGATIVE

1 Listen and repeat.

She doesn't understand computers so she doesn't send e-mails.

2 Match the two parts of these sentences.

She walks to work	they don't come to the office.
They're at the ticket office	because she doesn't have a car.
He doesn't understand Olga	so he doesn't work after 3:00.
On Sundays	because they don't have tickets.
He arrives at the office at 7:30	because he doesn't speak Russian.

CHECK Positive and negative

+	−
I **speak** English.	I **don't speak** English.
He **speaks** English.	He **doesn't speak** English.

For more, go to page 82.

THEY DO, THEY DON'T

3 Put the verbs in brackets ( ) into the correct form. Then listen and check.

1 He's a customer. He (not sell) things, he (buy) things.
He doesn't sell things, he buys things.

2 We're factory workers. We (not work) for a supermarket, we (work) for a manufacturing company.

____

3 I'm a salesperson. I (not manage) people, I (sell) things.

____

4 It's a charity. It (not make) things, it (help) people.

____

SHORT ANSWERS

4 Listen and repeat.

Do you speak English? — Yes, I do. / No, I don't.

Does she understand? — Yes, she does. / No, she doesn't.

5 Tick (✓) the correct answer.

1 Do you sell maps?
- *a* Yes, we are. *b* Yes, we can. *c* Yes, we do. ✓

2 Is it a charity?
- *a* No, it isn't. *b* No, it can't. *c* No, it doesn't.

3 Does she manage people?
- *a* Yes, she do. *b* Yes, she does. *c* Yes, she is.

4 Can I buy a ticket, please?
- *a* Yes, you do. *b* Yes, you can. *c* Yes, you can't.

5 Do they make cars?
- *a* No, they do. *b* No, they aren't. *c* No, they don't.

NOW YOU

6 Write sentences about yourself, using the positive or negative form of the present simple.

I don't smoke.

______ drink coffee.

______ understand American TV.

______ have a mobile phone.

______ go to restaurants.

______ speak Russian.

7 Take turns to ask and answer questions.

Do you smoke? — *No, I don't.*

Does she smoke? — *Yes, she does.*

real world *Introductions*

INTRODUCING YOURSELF

1 Here are three ways of introducing yourself. Match them to the situations.

Dear Anna, My name's Peter.	in a meeting
Hello, Anna, it's Peter here.	in an e-mail
Hello, I'm Peter.	on the phone

INTRODUCING OTHERS

2 Listen and repeat.

3 Work in groups of three. **A** Introduce B and C to each other, using the phrases above. Then swap roles.

AT A PARTY

4 Listen to the conversation and complete the table.

What are their names?	*Peter*	*Anna*
What do they do?		
Who do they work for?	*Silverchip*	*AJ.com*
What kinds of company are they?		
What do the companies do?		

5 Take turns to ask and answer questions about Peter and Anna.

AN E-MAIL INTRODUCTION

6 Imagine that you receive this e-mail. Fill the gaps with information about yourself: your name, your country, your job, your company.

From: Jordan Liu
To: __________
Subject: Information about you

Hi __________

Thank you for your e-mail. Before we meet, can I have some more information about you?

You say you are from __________ and you are a __________ , but what do you do in this job?

You also say you work for __________ . I'm sorry, but I don't know this company. What kind of company is it? Where are its offices?

Can we meet at my office on Thursday or Friday?

Regards,

Jordan Liu

7 Write a reply to the e-mail. Answer the questions and fix a time for the meeting.

A BUSINESS CARD

8 Look at the business card.

A Ask B these questions.
B Say the answers.

What does he do?
Where does he work?
What's his fax number?

B Ask A these questions.
A Say the answers.

Who does he work for?
What's his e-mail address?
What's his phone number?

Yadoo

Kim Jo Pak SALES MANAGER
Yadoo
Yadoo Building
Pusan

E-mail: jopak@yadoo.co.ko
Tel: 008 251 317324
Fax: 008 251 891254

CHECK E-mail

@ = at
• = dot

NOW YOU

9 Write a business card for yourself (or use your real business card) and give it to your teacher. Ask and answer questions about the people on the business cards your teacher gives to you.

review 3

VOCABULARY
Wordsearch

1 Go down ↓ and across → to find 14 words from Units 5 and 6 in this square. (You can find wordlists on pages 102–103.)

M	A	N	A	G	E	F	P	C
A	R	P	W	S	E	L	L	H
K	A	B	O	U	T	I	A	A
E	A	I	R	P	O	R	T	R
B	U	Y	K	N	O	W	F	I
O	D	H	E	L	P	X	O	T
S	E	C	R	E	T	A	R	Y
S	I	X	T	E	E	N	M	Z

GRAMMAR CHECK
Present simple

2 Write questions and answers. Put the verbs in brackets ( ) into the correct form.

1 How (you go) to work? *How do you go to work?*
I (go) to work by bus. *I go to work by bus.*
2 Where (he work)? ______
He (work) in Manila. ______
3 What time (she come) to the office? ______
She (come) to the office at 9:30. ______
4 Where (they live)? ______
They (live) in Ankara. ______
5 How (they go) to New York? ______
They (fly) to New York. ______

3 Make these sentences negative.

1 I go to work by train. *I don't go to work by train.*
2 You smoke cigars. ______
3 He has an office in Kiev. ______
4 She lives in Cairo. ______
5 We speak Japanese. ______

PRONUNCIATION
Thirteen or thirty?

4 Listen and write down the numbers. Compare your numbers with a partner.

5 Take turns to read and write down lists of numbers.

A Turn to page 75. **B** Turn to page 78.

FOCUS ON ...
Telling the time

6 Look at these ways of telling the time.

12:15	twelve fifteen	quarter past twelve
12:30	twelve thirty	half past twelve
12:45	twelve forty-five	quarter to one

7 Match these times.

1:30	5:30
quarter to six	quarter past two
seven fifteen	3:45
five thirty	five forty-five
2:15	one thirty
three forty-five	quarter past seven

8 Label this picture.

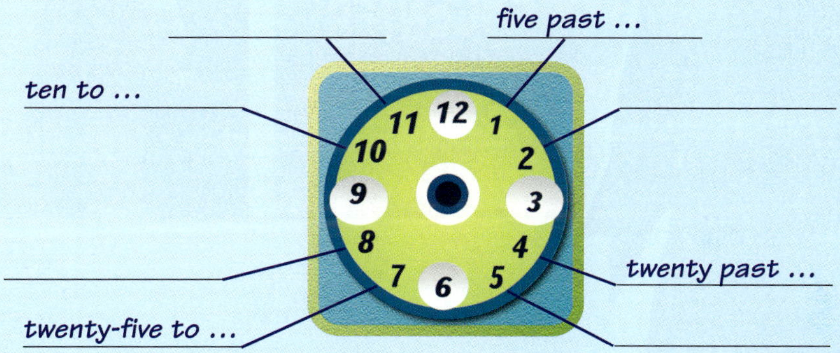

9 Write the time under these clocks.

10 Listen and write down the times. Compare your answers with a partner. Then listen again to check.

7 products

COMPANIES QUIZ

1 Answer the questions. Write these words in the 'Product' column.

coffee **clothes** **paintings** **computers** **cars** **food**

	ADJECTIVE	PRODUCT
1 What does Nestlé make?	*good*	*coffee*
2 What does WalMart sell?		
3 What does Ferrari make?		
4 What does Palm make?		
5 What does Christie's sell?		
6 What does Yves St Laurent make?		

2 Choose an adjective from the box to describe each of the products above and write it in the 'Adjective' column. (Use a dictionary to help you.)

good **small** **cheap** **fast** **old** **beautiful**

3 Match the adjectives above to their opposites.

bad	*good*	modern	______
expensive	______	ugly	______
slow	______	big	______

4 Listen and check. Then repeat.

RADIO ADVERTISEMENTS

5 Listen to two radio advertisements. Then fill the gaps with adjectives from the opposite page.

Computer Hut
Number one for business

Computer Hut is the number one shop for business computers. Do you work for a *big* company? Then come to Computer Hut. We have ________ , ________ computers for the ________ office. Do you travel for business? Then come to Computer Hut. We have ________ computers for the train, car and plane. Oh … and we're not ________ .

Computers for your business, in the office, train and plane. Computers are our business. Computer Hut's our name.

Sasha Noir

Hi. I'm a ________ woman and I like ________ clothes. So I buy my clothes at Sasha Noir. I like Sasha Noir's clothes because they're ________ . And also … I like them because they're ________ .

Sasha Noir. ________ clothes for ________ women.

I LIKE …

6 Write sentences about three products that you like and say why you like them. Use the adjectives on the opposite page.

I like Apple computers because they're fast.

I like … because they're …

7 Now write sentences about products that you don't like.

I don't like Ferrari cars because they're expensive.

I don't like … because they're …

NOW YOU

8 Take turns to ask and answer questions about products.

Do you like Gucci clothes?

Yes, I do. — *No, I don't.*

Why do you like them? — *Why not?*

Because they're … — *Because they're …*

GRAMMAR Comparatives

BIGGER OR SMALLER?

1 True or false? Write T or F next to the sentences.

1 Car A is bigger than car B. F
2 Car B is slower than car A.
3 Car A is more expensive than car B.
4 Car B is more modern than car A.
5 Car A is uglier than car B.
6 Car B is worse than car A.

2 Write five more sentences about the two cars. Use the comparatives in the box.

1 Car A is ________ than car B.
2 Car B is ________ than car A.
3 Car B is ________ than car A.
4 Car A is ________ than car B.
5 Car A is ________ than car B.
6 Car A is ________ than car B.

smaller
cheaper
older
faster
better
more beautiful

3 Take turns to ask and answer questions about the two cars.

Which car is smaller? — *Car A.*
Which car is bigger? — *Car B.*

CHECK Comparatives

When adjectives have one syllable, add *-er* for the comparative.
cheap — cheap**er**

When adjectives have two or more syllables, put ***more*** before the adjective.
expensive — **more** expensive

When adjectives end in *-y*, put *-ier* at the end of the adjective.
ugly — ugl**ier**

Some adjectives are irregular.
good — **better** — bad — **worse**

For more, go to page 80.

AN ADVERTISEMENT

4 Read this advertisement for a supermarket and answer the questions.

1 In what ways is Friselli worse than some other supermarkets?

2 In what ways is it better?

Friselli

COME TO FRISELLI!

FOOD FOR REAL PEOPLE!

At Friselli, we know the supermarket business. We know that some supermarkets are bigger than Friselli; we know that some are more modern. People say that some supermarkets have better salespeople and that some have faster service. So why do hundreds of people come to our shop every day? Because at Friselli, we also know that our food is always cheaper!

NOW YOU

5 Compare the two paintings. Use the comparatives on these pages.

Painting A is smaller than painting B.

A

B

6 Ask and answer questions about other products. You can talk about clothes, computers, food, mobile phones …

Are Apple computers better than Dell computers?

Yes, they are.

No, they aren't.

real world *Buying and selling*

WHAT DO YOU WANT?

1 What do you say in these situations? Write sentences. Use *I want …* .

SITUATION	WHAT DO YOU SAY?
1 The car is very small.	*I want a bigger one.*
2 The ticket is very expensive.	
3 The computer is very slow.	
4 The mobile phone is very big.	
5 The painting is very ugly.	
6 The hotel room is very old.	

CHECK *want* + noun

I **want a** car.
I **want a** bigger one.

For more, go to page 84.

WHAT DO YOU WANT TO DO?

CHECK *want to* + verb

I **want to** go.

For more, go to page 84.

2 Answer these questions.
Use the words in brackets ( ) to make sentences.

1 She's a businesswoman. What does she want to do? (make money)
She wants to make money.

2 You're in a supermarket. What do you want to buy? (buy food)
____

3 He's a car salesman. What does he want to do? (sell cars)
____

4 They're at the airport. Where do they want to go? (go to Singapore)
____

5 She's at her computer. What does she want to do? (send an e-mail)
____

6 He's on the phone. What does he want to do? (speak to his customer)
____

A BUSINESS SUIT

3 Listen to a conversation between a salesperson and a customer. Then fill the gaps with these phrases.

■ SALESPERSON

Do you like this one? **do you want?**
Can I help you?

○ CUSTOMER

It's very expensive. **I want to buy**
Do you have a bigger one?
Can I have it, please? **How much is it?**

■ Good morning, sir. ___________
○ Yes. ___________ a suit.
■ What kind of suit ___________
○ I want a good, modern business suit.
■ How about this one, sir? ___________
○ Oh, yes. Yes, I do. ___________
■ $990, sir.
○ Oh. ___________ Do you have a cheaper one?
■ Oh, yes, sir. We have a good suit for $199.
○ Can I try it on?
■ Of course, sir … So, how is it, sir?
○ Well, it's very small. ___________
■ No, I'm sorry, sir, we don't.
○ But it is very, very cheap. I want it. ___________

NOW YOU

4 Role play these situations. Use the phrases in the boxes above and others that you know.

- **A** You go to B's shop because you want to buy a mobile phone. Turn to page 75.
  B You work in a shop that sells mobile phones. Turn to page 78.
- **B** You phone A because you want to buy a computer. Turn to page 78.
  A You are a computer salesperson. Turn to page 75.

8 bookings

HOTEL WORDS

1 Look at the clues and complete the word puzzle. (Use a dictionary to help you.)

Across ▶

2 

4 

6  ___ room

8  ___ service

Down ▼

1  ___ room

3  ___ pool

5 

7 

2 Listen and check. Then repeat.

BOOKING A HOTEL

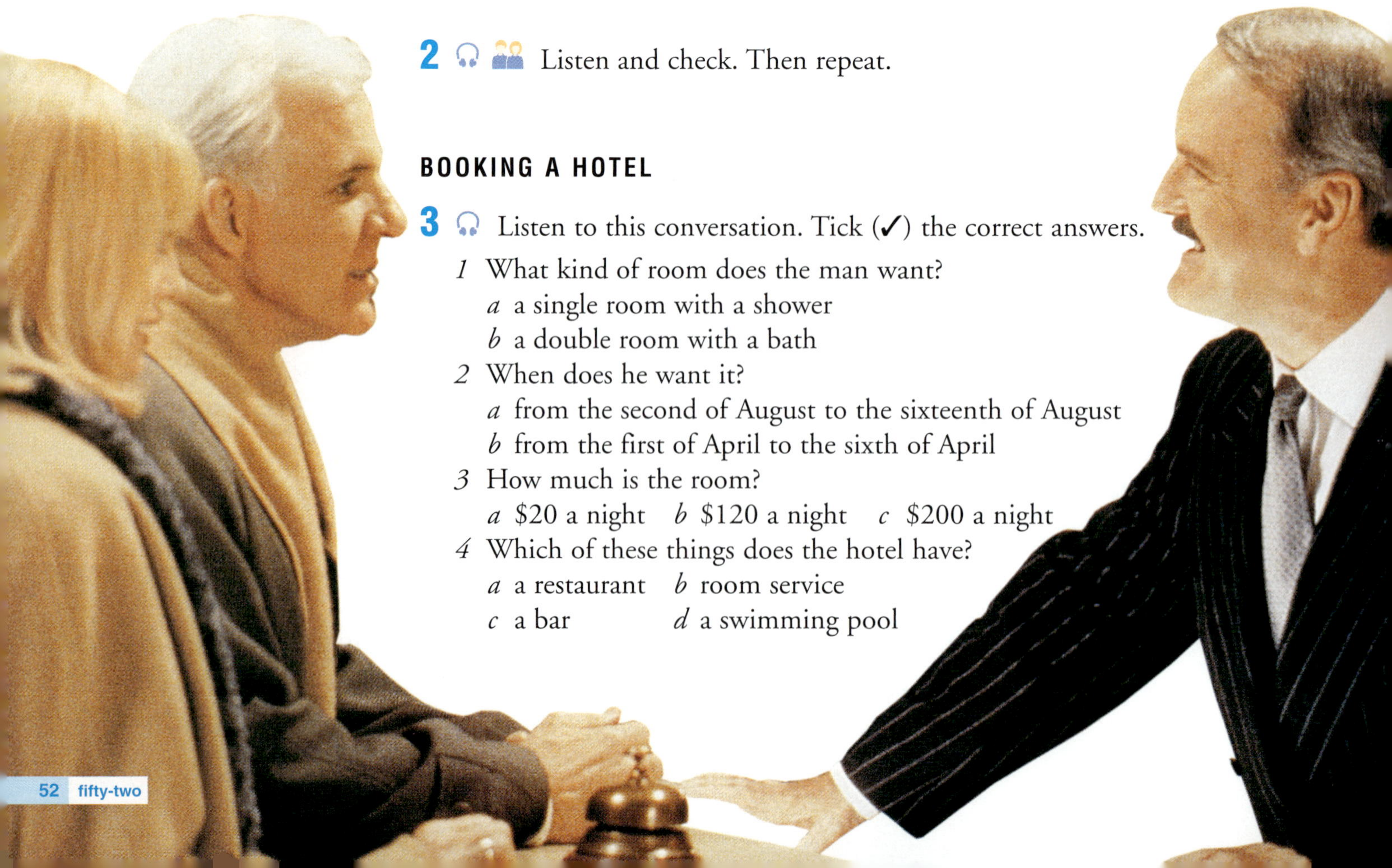

3 Listen to this conversation. Tick (✓) the correct answers.

1 What kind of room does the man want?
   a a single room with a shower
   b a double room with a bath

2 When does he want it?
   a from the second of August to the sixteenth of August
   b from the first of April to the sixth of April

3 How much is the room?
   a \$20 a night *b* \$120 a night *c* \$200 a night

4 Which of these things does the hotel have?
   a a restaurant *b* room service
   c a bar *d* a swimming pool

DATES

4 Match the numbers and the words.

2nd	thirty-first
17th	second
10th	ninth
23rd	seventeenth
31st	tenth
9th	twenty-third

5 Listen and repeat these months.

January	February	March	April	May	June
July	August	September	October	November	December

6 Write these dates as numbers.

the seventh of November	7/11	the third of March	______
the fourteenth of May	______	the eighteenth of February	______
the twenty-fifth of December	______	the thirtieth of June	______

7 Write these numbers as dates.

2/10   3/8   21/4   19/1   5/7   26/9

RENTING A CAR

8 Listen to the telephone conversation. Tick (✓) the correct answers.

1 What kind of car does he want?
  a He wants a small, fast car.
  b He wants a big, fast car.
2 When does he want it?
  a from 26 May to 7 June
  b from 27 May to 6 June
3 How much is it?
  a $65 a day   *b* $175 a day

NOW YOU

9 Take turns to ask and answer questions about these bookings.

Example: Car Seoul 26/6–2/7

When do you want the car in Seoul?

From the twenty-sixth of June to the second of July.

Car Lisbon 14/4–21/4
Hotel Athens 7/2–12/2
Car Cairo 17/8–3/9
Hotel Singapore 22/10–1/11

GRAMMAR *there is … there are …*

A HOTEL WEBSITE

1 Read this information about the Cosmo Hotel and tick (✓) the correct answers to the questions below.

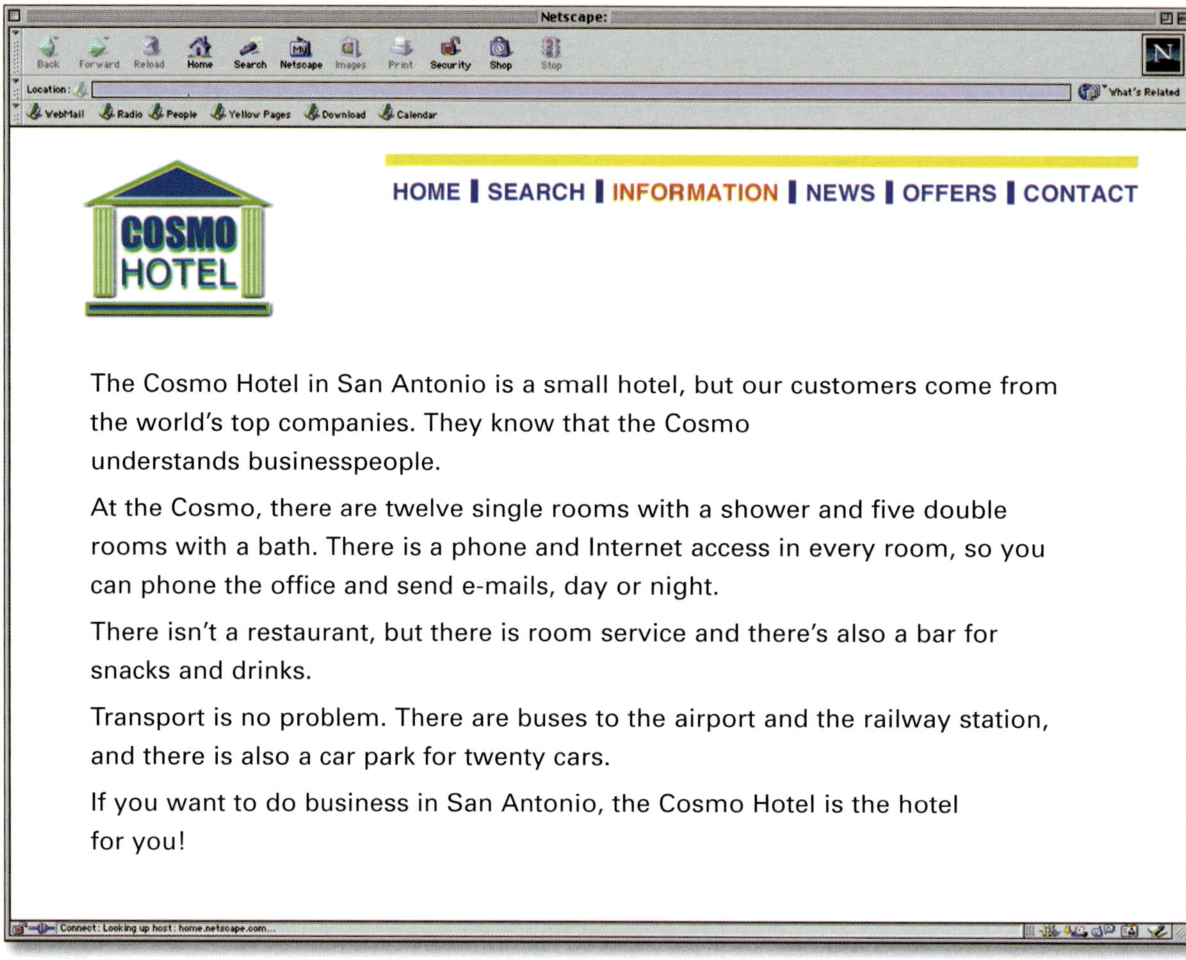

COSMO HOTEL

HOME | SEARCH | INFORMATION | NEWS | OFFERS | CONTACT

The Cosmo Hotel in San Antonio is a small hotel, but our customers come from the world's top companies. They know that the Cosmo understands businesspeople.

At the Cosmo, there are twelve single rooms with a shower and five double rooms with a bath. There is a phone and Internet access in every room, so you can phone the office and send e-mails, day or night.

There isn't a restaurant, but there is room service and there's also a bar for snacks and drinks.

Transport is no problem. There are buses to the airport and the railway station, and there is also a car park for twenty cars.

If you want to do business in San Antonio, the Cosmo Hotel is the hotel for you!

1 Are there any single rooms with a bath?
a Yes, there are. *b* No, there aren't.

2 Are there any double rooms with a bath?
a Yes, there are. *b* No, there aren't.

3 Can you send e-mails from your room?
a Yes, you can. *b* No, you can't.

4 Is there a restaurant?
a Yes, there is. *b* No, there isn't.

5 Can you have meals in your room?
a Yes, you can. *b* No, you can't.

6 Is there a bar?
a Yes, there is. *b* No, there isn't.

7 Is there a bus to the airport?
a Yes, there is. *b* No, there isn't.

CHECK *there is … there are …*

Singular
There is a restaurant.
There isn't a restaurant.
Is there a restaurant?

Plural
There are two restaurants.
There aren't any restaurants.
Are there any restaurants?

For more, go to page 83.

THE GRAND HOTEL

2 Write sentences about The Grand Hotel. Use *There is …* or *There are …* and these phrases.

The Grand Hotel

- near the beach
- 45 double rooms with a bath or a shower
- 32 single rooms with a shower
- 2 restaurants
- 3 bars
- room service
- a swimming pool

The Grand Hotel is a big, old hotel near the beach. There are forty-five double rooms with …

ASKING FOR INFORMATION

3 Listen and then fill the gaps with these phrases.

is there a **there is a** **there are some** **Are there any**

■ Good evening. The Ritz Hotel.
○ Good evening. Can I book a room, please?
■ Yes, of course.
○ ___________ double rooms with a bath?
■ No, but there are some double rooms with a shower.
○ And are there any single rooms with a bath?
■ No, I'm sorry, there aren't. But, of course, ___________ single rooms with a shower.
○ Good. Is there a restaurant?
■ No, there isn't, but ___________ bar.
○ And ___________ swimming pool?
■ Yes, there is.
○ Thank you.

CHECK *some* and *any*

Singular
+ There is a room.
– There isn't a room.

Plural
+ **There are some** rooms.
– **There aren't any** rooms.

For more, go to page 83.

NOW YOU

4 Look at your description of The Grand Hotel above. Take turns to ask and answer questions about it, and about the Cosmo and other hotels that you know.

Is there a … ? *Are there any … ?*

real world *Online and telephone bookings*

BOOKING ONLINE

1 Look at the web page and answer these questions.

1 You want to book a hotel room. Where do you click?
2 You don't understand the web page. Where do you click?
3 You want to go from JFK Airport to Wall Street, but you don't know New York. Where do you click?
4 You want to book a plane ticket. Where do you click?
5 You want information about restaurants in Tokyo. What do you do?

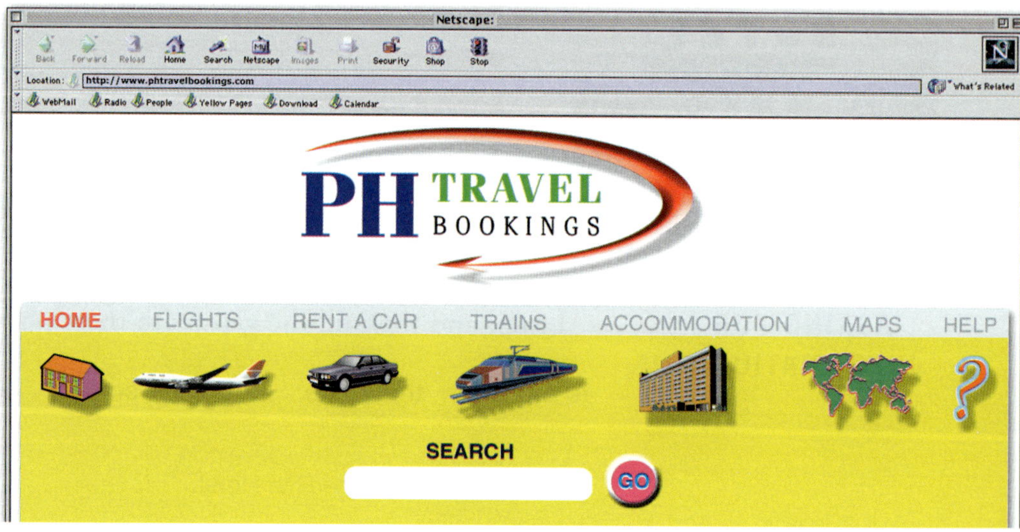

BOOKING A BUSINESS TRIP

2 Listen and put the missing information on these web pages.

1

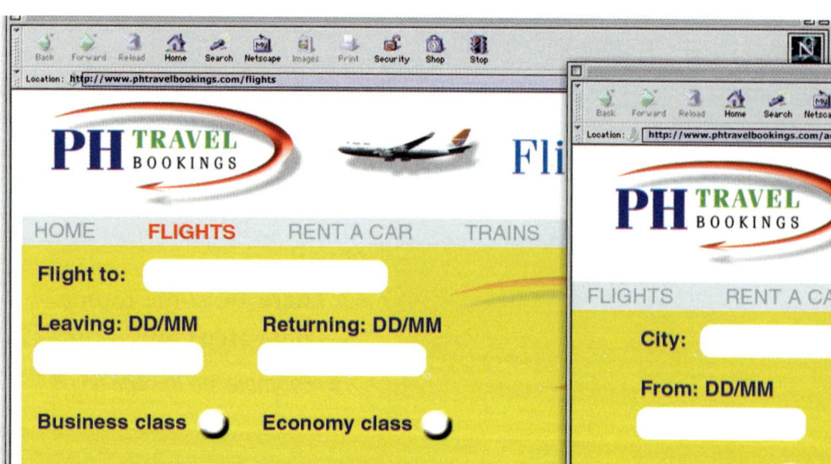

2

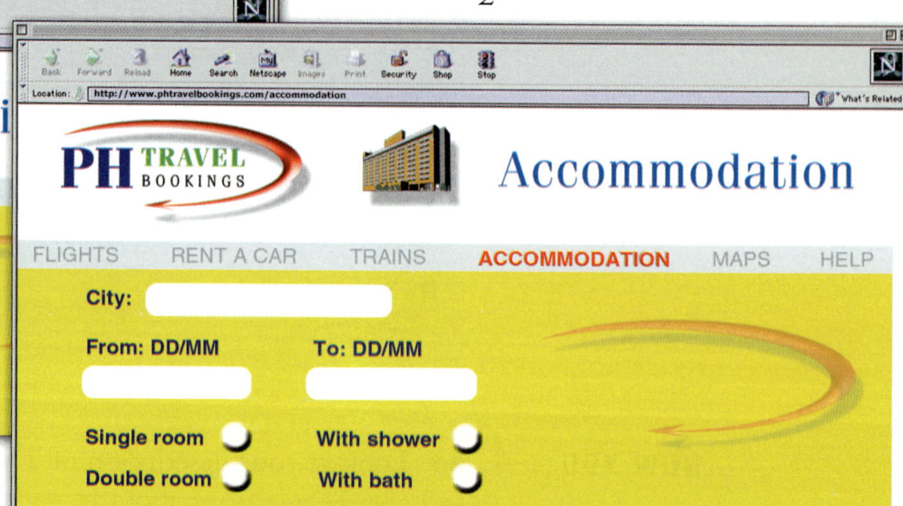

BOOKING ROLES

3 Take turns to phone and book a hotel room. **A** Turn to page 76. **B** Turn to page 79. Use these phrases and others that you know.

TRAVEL AGENT

What kind of room do you want?

When do you want the room?

CUSTOMER

I want to book a hotel room.

How much is it?

Is there a restaurant / a swimming pool / a gym?

4 Take turns to play the roles of customer and travel agent again. **A** Turn to page 76. **B** Turn to page 79. Use these phrases and others that you know.

TRAVEL AGENT

When do you want to leave?

When do you want to return?

What kind of car do you want?

CUSTOMER

I want to book a flight.

I want to rent a car.

I want to book a train ticket.

NOW YOU

5 You want to make a trip – a holiday or a business trip. Think about these questions.

Where do you want to go?
How do you want to travel?
When do you want to go?
What kind of hotel do you want?

6 Take turns to be the customer and travel agent. Ask and answer questions about your trips.

7 Go to a travel website on the Internet. What do you do to book your trip online?

review 4

VOCABULARY
Collocations

1 Which words go together? Look at Units 7 and 8 to help you.

car	service	*car park*
boarding	office	________
room	pool	________
mobile	station	________
web	page	________
double	agent	________
travel	room	________
swimming	park	________
railway	phone	________
ticket	gate	________

GRAMMAR CHECK
Comparatives and *there is … / there are …*

2 Complete the table.

ADJECTIVE	COMPARATIVE
small	*smaller*
	bigger
beautiful	
	cheaper
fast	
	more modern
expensive	
	uglier
good	
	worse

3 Match the two parts of these sentences.

There is	any trains today.
There are	any double rooms?
There aren't	a gym.
Are there	some tickets.

PRONUNCIATION
Sound and spelling

4 Listen to these pairs of words. Do the underlined letters sound the same (✓) or different (✗)?

bar	–	bath	✓	web	–	better	
modern	–	company		go	–	old	
want	–	bad		click	–	big	
please	–	meeting		but	–	June	
good	–	food		suit	–	you	

FOCUS ON …
Big numbers and dates

5 Listen and repeat.

1,000	one thousand	30,465	thirty thousand four hundred and sixty-five
2,000	two thousand		
100,000	one hundred thousand	406,512	four hundred and six thousand five hundred and twelve
1,000,000	one million		
1,040	one thousand and forty		
2,007	two thousand and seven	1,000,059	one million and fifty-nine

6 Write these as numbers.

1 seven thousand four hundred and forty-six 7,446
2 ten thousand six hundred ______
3 one hundred thousand ______
4 five thousand eight hundred and twenty ______
5 sixteen thousand two hundred and four ______
6 nineteen thousand and ninety-one ______

7 Take turns to say these numbers. Then listen and check.

42,000 150,000 6,400 1,000,000 9,999 12,666
500,520 17,177

8 Look at how to say these dates.

6 June 2006 the sixth of June two thousand and six
17 December 2010 the seventeenth of December two thousand and ten

9 Take turns to say these dates. Then listen and check.

12th May 2004 11/11/09 October 26 2018
31st August 2025 3rd January 2019 19/09/08

NOTES

1 For the year 2010, say: *two thousand and ten*
For the year 1998, say: *nineteen ninety-eight*

2 In the UK and Europe, the day is first, then the month and then the year.
In the USA, the month is first, then the day and then the year.
9th April 2007
= 09/04/07 (UK)
= 04/09/07 (US)

9 directions

INSIDE AND OUTSIDE

1 Which of these things are normally inside a building and which are normally outside? Write the words in the correct group. (Use a dictionary to help you.)

pavement **lift** **toilets**
cashpoint **underground station**
corridor **ground floor**

inside

outside

2 Six of the words or phrases above are different in US English. Use a dictionary to help you match the British English words above with the US English words in the box.

first floor **subway station** **ATM**
restrooms **sidewalk** **elevator**

3 Listen and check. Then repeat.

US/UK QUIZ

4 Use words from page 60 to answer the questions in this quiz.

1. You want to get a train in London. Where do you go? ______________
2. You want to get some money in Los Angeles. Where do you go? ______________
3. You want to go from the ground floor to the sixteenth floor in Edinburgh. How do you go? ______________
4. When you're outside in New York, what do you walk on? ______________
5. A British person says 'the fourth floor'. What does an American person call the same thing? ______________

PREPOSITIONS

5 Look at these words and pictures. Then listen to three conversations and answer the questions below.

1 What is at the end of the corridor? ______________
2 What is next to the bar? ______________
3 Where is the car? ______________

NOW YOU

6 Look at these pictures. Take turns to ask and answer questions. (You can use British or US English!)

Where's the underground station?

It's at the corner of the street.

GRAMMAR Imperatives

SIGNS

1 Write these directions under the correct signs.

Go straight down the road. **Take the third on the right.**
Don't turn right. **Take the second on the left.** **Don't turn left.**

1

Go straight down the road.

2

____

3

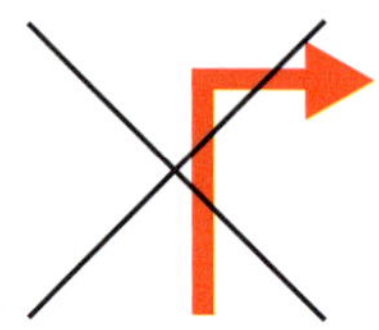

____

4

____

5

____

CHECK Imperatives

+	−
Turn left.	**Don't turn** right.

For more, go to page 80.

GIVING DIRECTIONS

2 Listen to a conversation in a hotel. Put these directions in the correct order.

Turn right. ☐
Go straight down the corridor. ☐
Room 201 is the seventh door on the left. ☐
Come out of the lift. ☐
Take the lift to the second floor. ☐

3 Compare your order with a partner.

PREPOSITIONS

4 Match these words to the pictures. (Use a dictionary to help you.)

into **round** **out of** **past** **across**

1

2

3

4

5

THREE MAPS

5 Fill the gaps with the prepositions opposite.

Go ________ the shop and turn right. Walk ________ the bank and ________ the bridge. Then go ________ the corner and ________ the park. The subway station is on your right.

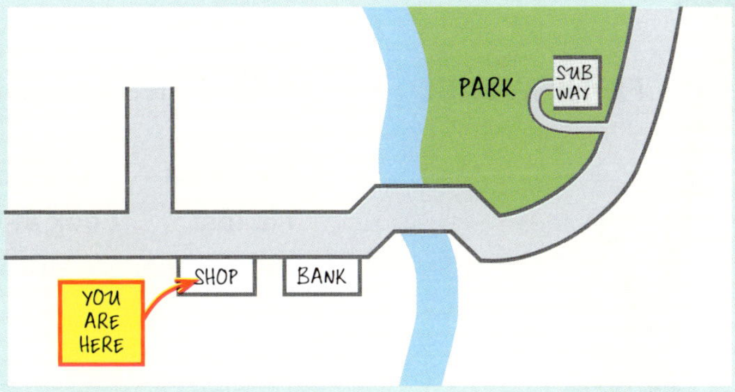

6 **A** Ask B *Where's the cashpoint?* **B** Give directions.
A Follow the route with your finger.

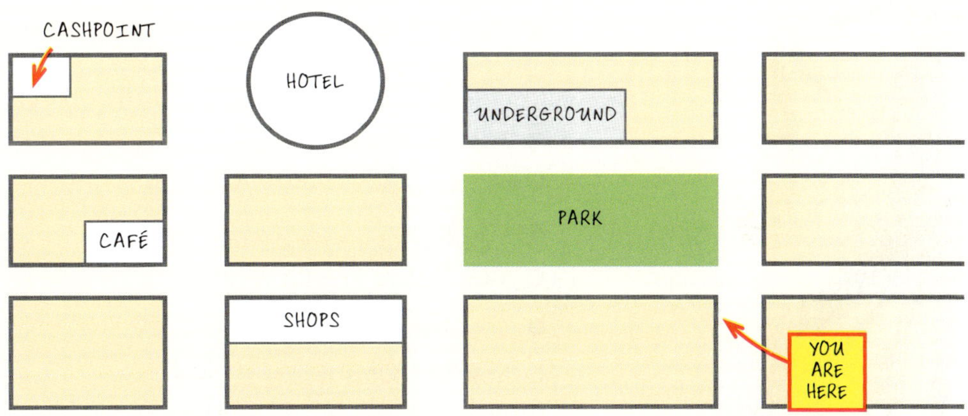

7 **B** Ask A *Where's the elevator?* **A** Give directions.
B Follow the route with your finger.

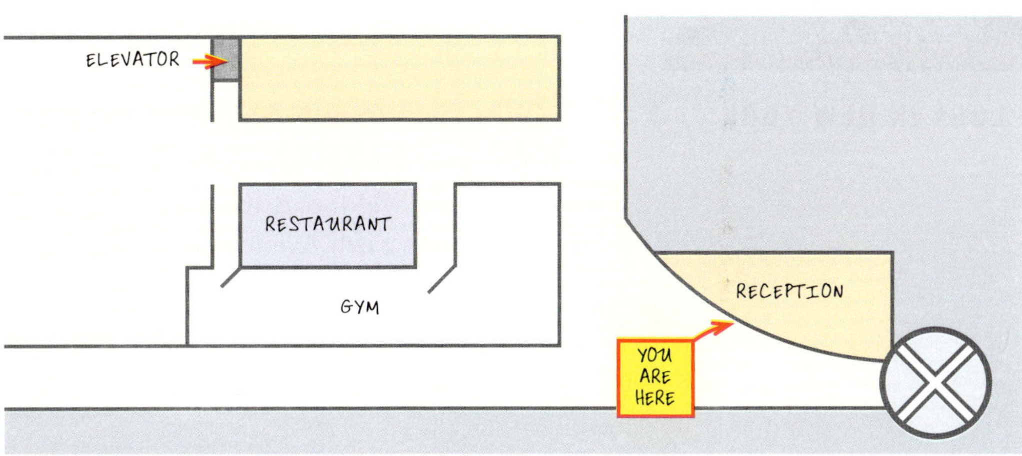

real world

Asking for and giving directions

FIFTH AVENUE

1 Listen and then fill the gaps with these phrases.

I'm afraid **What do you mean?**
I'm lost. **Look at the sign.**
Excuse me. **How do I get there?**

■ __________
○ Yes?
■ __________ Where's Fifth Avenue?
○ Fifth Avenue?
■ Yes, is it near here?
○ Yes, it is.
■ Oh, good. __________
○ __________ I can't help you.
■ I'm sorry. __________
○ Well, you're in Fifth Avenue.
■ You mean, this is Fifth Avenue?
○ Yes, of course it is. __________
■ Fifth Avenue! Thank you! Now, where are the shops?

2 Read the conversation.

LOST IN NEW YORK

3 Look at the map of New York opposite and listen to the directions. Follow the route with your finger. Where do the directions take you?

1 Go out of the Waldorf Astoria … __________
2 Go out of Saks Fifth Avenue … __________

4 Take turns to ask for and give the directions above.

UPPER MIDTOWN NEW YORK

NOW YOU **5** Look at the map of New York again. Take turns to ask for and give directions to these places.

A Ask for directions from the Trump Tower to the Waldorf Astoria.
B Give the directions.

B Ask for directions from Lever House to Saks Fifth Avenue.
A Give the directions.

10 problems

TRAVEL PROBLEMS

1 Look at this information board and answer the questions.

FLIGHT NO.	DEPARTURES	
AF 10711	Marseilles	Go to check-in
SA 45011	Cape Town	Delayed
BA 43210	Sydney	Cancelled
MO 65438	Riyadh	Go to check-in
KLM 874	Delhi	Boarding
VA 97689	Houston	Final call

1 Which flight is the first to leave? ________
2 Which flight is the second to leave? ________
3 Which flight is late? ________
4 Which flight can't people take? ________

2 Fill the gaps in the conversations with these phrases.

it's cancelled. **I'm late.** **Go straight to the boarding gate.**
Can I have some information **Do you want to wait in the lounge?**
when's the next flight? **Can I check in** **Don't worry.**

1

■ Good morning.
○ Good morning. ________ for the flight to Delhi, please?
■ The flight to Delhi?
○ Yes, I'm sorry. I know ________
■ ________ Here's your boarding pass. ________
○ Thank you.

2

■ Excuse me. ________ about the flight to Sydney, please? BA 43210.
○ BA 43210. Oh. I'm afraid ________
■ Well, ________
○ Tomorrow morning at 6:00.
■ Tomorrow morning!
○ Yes. I'm sorry. ________
■ What? Wait in the lounge!

3 Listen and check.

MONEY PROBLEMS

4 Complete the sentences with these words. (Use a dictionary to help you.)

currency **cash** **credit card** **cheque**

1 Dollars, yen and euros are kinds of ____________ .
2 Visa and Mastercard are ____________ companies.
3 Banknotes and coins are ____________ .
4 A bank gives its customers a ____________ book.

5 Choose one of these questions for each of the situations in the table.

Can I pay by credit card? **Can I write a cheque?**
Can I change some money?

SITUATION	QUESTION
1 You want to pay some money to a friend, but you don't have any cash.	
2 You are on a business trip and you want some currency.	
3 You want to buy something in a shop, but you don't have any cash.	

6 Listen to a conversation in a hotel and answer these questions.

1 What does the woman want to do? Tick (✓) the correct answer.
  a She wants to check in.
  b She wants to check out.

2 How does she want to pay? ____________

3 Why can't she do this? Tick (✓) the correct answer.
  a She doesn't have enough money.
  b There's a problem with the machine.

4 How does she solve the problem? ____________

NOW YOU

7 Role play these situations.

- **A** You are at the airport and you want to check in for a flight to Buenos Aires.
  B Turn to page 79.
- **B** You want to check out of your hotel (room 872).
  A Turn to page 76.

GRAMMAR Asking questions

QUESTION WORDS

1 Match the questions and answers.

When can we meet?	He's my boss.
Why do you come to work by car?	It's $1,000.
Who is the old man in your office?	I'm a salesman.
How much is it?	It's next to the supermarket.
What do you do?	It's a bank.
Which company do you work for?	Fine, thank you.
How are you?	Because there aren't any trains.
Where is your office?	How about nine o'clock on Tuesday?
What kind of company is it?	I work for IBM.

2 Fill the gaps in the questions. Use the words in **bold** above.

- ■ Hi, Carl. _____'s the problem?
- ○ Hi. I'm late for the meeting.
- ■ _____ does it start?
- ○ Nine thirty.
- ■ Nine thirty? It's nine thirty now! _____'s the meeting with?
- ○ It's with my boss and her boss! Now, _____'s meeting room two?
- ■ It's on the second floor at the end of the corridor.
- ○ _____ floor?
- ■ The second floor!

3 Listen and check.

HOW BAD IS IT?

4 Listen and complete these five questions that Ground Control asks.

1 What *'s the situation* ?

2 How ______________ ?

3 How ______________ ?

4 What ______________ ?

5 How ______________ ?

5 Listen again. What are Major Tom's answers to the questions above?

6 Write questions with *How* in the right-hand column.

YOU WANT TO KNOW ...	WHAT DO YOU SAY?
1 Is your company big or small?	*How big is your company?*
2 Are your products expensive or cheap?	
3 Are your products good or bad?	
4 Is your service fast or slow?	
5 Is your office old or modern?	

7 Take turns to ask and answer the questions above.

How big is your company?

It's very big. Ten thousand people work for it.

It's not very big. Only ten people work for it.

CHECK *How* + adjective + verb

How old are you?
How expensive is it?

NOW YOU

8 Take turns to ask and answer questions about yourselves and other people in the class. Use questions like the ones on these pages and others that you know. You can ask about jobs, companies, apartments, cars, computers and anything else you like!

real world *Messages*

AN ANSWERPHONE MESSAGE

1 Listen to a message on an answerphone and answer these questions.

1 What time is it and what day is it?

Time: ______ Day: ______

2 What is Katie's problem? Tick (✓) the correct answer.

a She's early. *b* She's late.

3 Where is she? ____________

4 What's her mobile phone number? ____________

5 What does she want Ravi to do? Tick (✓) the correct answer.

a Cancel the meeting. *b* Wait for her.
c Start the meeting without her.

ANSWERPHONE WORDS

2 Listen and fill the gaps in the message with these words.

tone answerphone ring afraid take leave a message

This is the ____________ for Ravi Shipman. I'm ____________ I can't ____________ your call at the moment, so please ____________ after the ____________ or ____________ my mobile on 07771 456321.

3 Now fill the same gaps with these words. Then listen and check.

bleep answer sorry voicemail call speak

This is the ____________ for Ravi Shipman. I'm ____________ I can't ____________ your call at the moment, so please ____________ after the ____________ or ____________ my office on 0787 56522.

4 Write a message for your voicemail or answerphone at home or at work. Then read it to your partner.

TXT MSG

5 When people send text messages on mobile phones, they often use abbreviations.

Example: text message → txt msg

Look at the text message on this phone. Write it in full – replace the abbreviations with the words/phrases in the box and add punctuation.

thank you	**message**	**your**
for	**I'm**	**the meeting**
see you	**as soon as possible**	
please		

NOW YOU

6 Take turns to leave answerphone messages. Say your name and the time and leave your phone number. Take notes as your partner reads their message. Then read out your notes for your partner to check.

A Turn to page 76. **B** Turn to page 79.

7 Write text messages. Use abbreviations, if you can. If you have mobile phones, use them! If you don't have mobile phones, write your messages on pieces of paper.

A Turn to page 76. **B** Turn to page 79.

When you get your message, try to guess the full forms of the abbreviations.

review 5

VOCABULARY
Crossword

1 Complete this crossword with words from Units 9 and 10. (You can find wordlists on page 104.)

Across ▶

1 You get cash here in the UK.

5 It goes up and down in the USA.

7 In the USA they're restrooms. What are they in the UK?

8 B is _____ A and C.

12 As soon as _____ .

14  _____ left.

15 Good, better. Bad, _____ .

Down ▼

1 You can get one from Access or Visa.

2 In the USA it's a sidewalk. What is it in the UK?

3 See you _____ week!

4 Meet me at the _____ of the street.

6 You leave messages on an _____phone

8 Another word for *tone*.

9 What do you do? = What's your _____ ?

10 You can write one when you want to give people money.

11 The opposite of *early*.

13 The opposite of *fast*.

PRONUNCIATION
***s* or *z*?**

2 Listen. Is the underlined sound in these words an *s* sound or a *z* sound? Write *s* or *z* next to each word.

as answer business solve days weeks message phrase excuse me outside

GRAMMAR CHECK
Imperatives, prepositions and question words

3 Write instructions for these signs.

 ____________  ____________

4 Match these prepositions to the pictures.

at the end of **between** **across** **round** **next to**

1 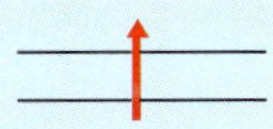 across
2  ________
3 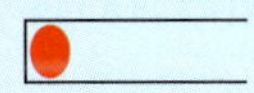 ________
4  ________
5  ________

5 Fill the gaps in these questions.

1	How old is your car?	It's very old.
2	_______ is the painting?	It's $20,000.
3	_______ is your boss?	She's in Frankfurt.
4	_______ computer do you want?	I want a cheap one, please.
5	_______ is the problem?	It's very bad.

FOCUS ON …
Abbreviations

6 Look at the documents and find abbreviations for these words and phrases.

morning **company** **please turn over** **Wednesday** **copies to**
Tuesday **number** **afternoon** **as soon as possible**

to hear the good news about the company in Japan. We are all

PTO

Hi Kate,

Thanks for the message. Can we meet on Tues pm?

Ravi

Wed am

Anna,
Please call Yusuf asap
His no. is: 809 8897

Best wishes,

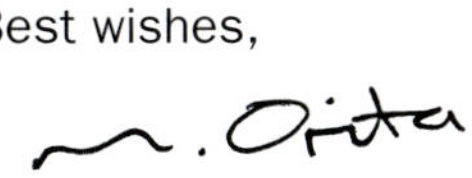

M. Orita
cc. Kim Jin Hiu
Leo van Zandt

PJ Harvey & Co

interactions

Student A

PHONE NUMBERS Unit 2 *page 10* exercise **7**

432-0536 31-32-10 2341-0610 132-4650

NOW YOU Unit 2 *page 11* exercise **12**

7 10 1 4 0 3 8 11 6

CHECKING NUMBERS Unit 2 *page 14* exercise **3**

2 3 5 8 10 11

NOW YOU Unit 2 *page 15* exercise **9**

MTA New York City Subway

Canal Street	$3	Central Avenue	$5
Canarsie Rockaway Parkway	$7	Chauncey Street	$3
Carroll Street	$3	City College	$3

NOW YOU Unit 3 *page 21* exercise **12**

Their names are Rupert and Wendi Murdoch. They're businesspeople. He's from Australia and she's from Hong Kong. The name of their company's News Corporation.

NOW YOU Unit 4 *page 27* exercise **8**

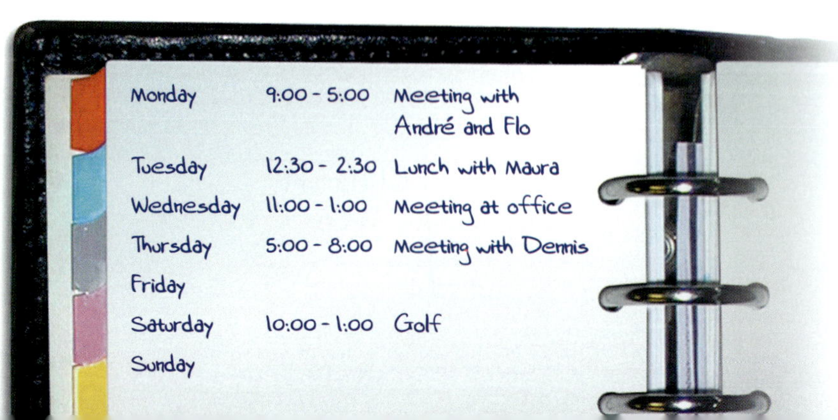

30 TO 100

Unit 5 *page 33* exercise **7**

Numbers: 66 35 16 87 41
Times: 12:45 23:25 7:30 11:15

NOW YOU

Unit 5 *page 35* exercise **10**

Thomas Costas is a teacher. He lives and works in Berlin. He goes to work on foot.

INFORMATION ROLES

Unit 5 *page 37* exercise **5**

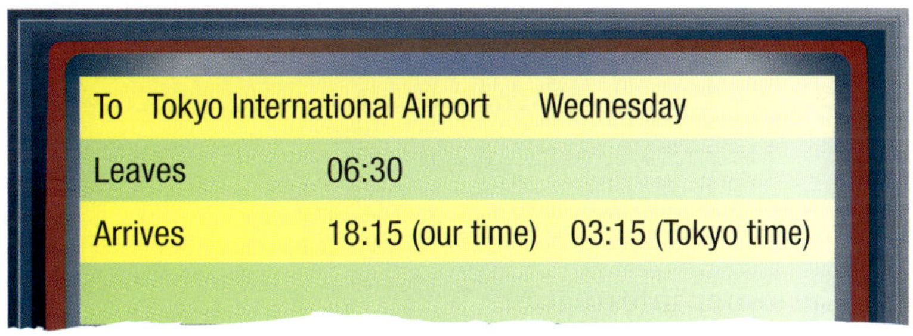

NOW YOU

Unit 5 *page 37* exercise **7**

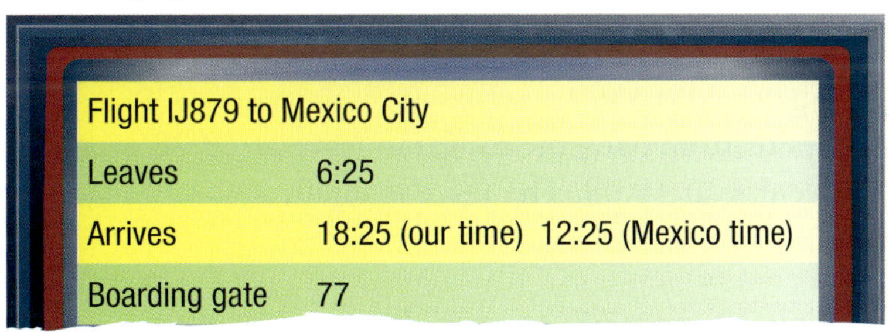

PRONUNCIATION

Review 3 *page 44* exercise **5**

40 60 18 70 15 16 13 30 90 19

NOW YOU

Unit 7 *page 51* exercise **4**

- You want to buy a small, modern mobile phone, but you only have $95.
- You have three kinds of computer:
  - a very small, very fast computer for $1,395
  - a very small, slower computer for $1,050
  - a bigger, slower computer for $760.

BOOKING ROLES

Unit 8 *page 57* exercise **3**

Customer information:
You want to book a double room with a shower in Shanghai from 21/11 to 7/12.

Travel agent information:

The Cosmo Hotel, Los Angeles

At the Cosmo Hotel in Los Angeles, there are fifteen double rooms with a bath and shower ($350 a night) and twenty-seven single rooms with a bath and shower ($250 a night). There is also a car park, a restaurant, a bar, room service and a small swimming pool.

COSMO HOTEL

BOOKING ROLES

Unit 8 *page 57* exercise **4**

Customer information:
You want to fly from your home town to Buenos Aires on 4/5 and return on 11/5. You want to rent a small car for a week in Argentina.

Travel agent information:
There are flights to Moscow every day at 12:15. They return every day at 15:30. The price is $599.
Trains from Moscow to Kazan leave at 19:28 every evening and return every evening at 19:08. The price is $200.

NOW YOU

Unit 10 *page 67* exercise **7**

Ask B his/her name and room number. Then say that there is a problem with the credit card machine and ask B how he/she wants to pay.

NOW YOU

Unit 10 *page 71* exercise **6**

Say you are lost in Fifth Avenue and ask B for directions. Ask B to call your mobile phone on 07676 898006.

NOW YOU

Unit 10 *page 71* exercise **7**

Write that you are sorry you are late for the meeting. Say that you are at the airport and tell B to start the meeting without you.

Student B

PHONE NUMBERS

Unit 2 *page 10* exercise **7**

10-14-35-41 6351-4231 041-2654 120-3645

NOW YOU

Unit 2 *page 11* exercise **12**

9 2 0 8 12 5 6 7 3

CHECKING NUMBERS

Unit 2 *page 14* exercise **3**

1 4 6 7 9 12

NOW YOU

Unit 2 *page 15* exercise **8**

DRINKS

Orange juice	€3
Cola	€2
Tea	€2
Coffee	€3

NOW YOU

Unit 3 *page 21* exercise **12**

Their names are Brent Hoberman and Martha Lane Fox. They're businesspeople from the UK. The name of their company's lastminute.com.

NOW YOU

Unit 4 *page 27* exercise **8**

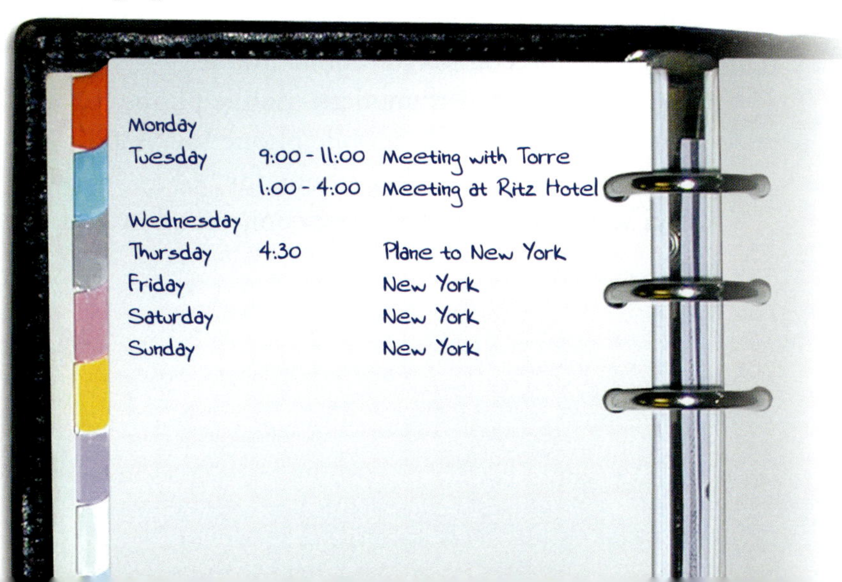

30 TO 100

Unit 5 *page 33* exercise **7**

Numbers: 13 31 99 86 56
Times: 3:20 14:20 22:50 19:35

NOW YOU

Unit 5 *page 35* exercise **10**

Patricia Harvey is a businesswoman. She lives in Hollywood and she works in Los Angeles. She goes to work by car.

INFORMATION ROLES

Unit 5 *page 37* exercise **5**

NOW YOU

Unit 5 *page 37* exercise **7**

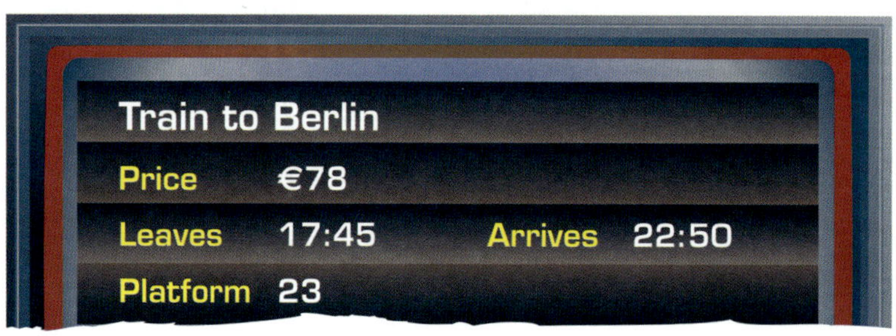

PRONUNCIATION

Review 3 *page 44* exercise **5**

17 70 80 18 16 13 15 50 60 20

NOW YOU

Unit 7 *page 51* exercise **4**

- You have three kinds of mobile phone:
  - a very small, very modern mobile phone for $145
  - a very small, older mobile phone for $105
  - a bigger, older mobile phone for $65.
- You want to buy a small, fast computer, but you only have $990.

BOOKING ROLES

Unit 8 *page 57* exercise **3**

Travel agent information:

The Cosmo Hotel, Shanghai

At the Cosmo Hotel in Shanghai, there are twelve double rooms with a shower ($300 a night) and twenty-two single rooms with a shower ($200 a night). There is also a car park, a restaurant, a bar and room service.

Customer information:
You want to book a single room with a bath in Los Angeles from 13/3 to 2/4.

BOOKING ROLES

Unit 8 *page 57* exercise **4**

Travel agent information:
There are flights to Buenos Aires every day at 06:20. They return every day at 19:40. The price is $1,299.
The price of a small car for a week in Argentina is $499.

Customer information:
You want to fly from your home town to Moscow on 22/6 and return on 29/6. You want to book a train ticket from Moscow to Kazan on 23/6 and return to Moscow on 27/6.

NOW YOU

Unit 10 *page 67* exercise **7**

You work at the airport. There is a two-hour delay on the flight to Buenos Aires. Ask A to wait in the lounge.

NOW YOU

Unit 10 *page 71* exercise **6**

Say you are sorry you are late for the meeting. Tell B to start without you and leave your mobile phone number – 08178 779451.

NOW YOU

Unit 10 *page 71* exercise **7**

Write that you are lost in Park Avenue. Ask A to send directions or call your mobile on 08178 779451.

grammar reference

ARTICLES

1 *a* or *an*?

an + a e i o u
a + b c d f g h j k l m n p q r s t v w x y z

SINGULAR	PLURAL
He's **a** student.	They're students.
They have **an** office in Madrid.	They have offices in many countries.

2 *a* or *the*?

What is it?	It's **a** train.
Which train is it?	It's **the** train to Paris.

CAN AND *CAN'T*

+	−	?
I can come	I can't come	Can I come?
You can come	You can't come	Can you come?
He can come	He can't come	Can he come?
She can come	She can't come	Can she come?
It can come	It can't come	Can it come?
We can come	We can't come	Can we come?
You can come	You can't come	Can you come?
They can come	They can't come	Can they come?

COMPARATIVE ADJECTIVES

When adjectives have one syllable, add *-er* for the comparative.
cheap cheap**er** big bigg**er**

When adjectives have two syllables and end in *-y*, add *-ier*.
easy eas**ier** ugly ugl**ier**

When adjectives have two or more syllables, put ***more*** before the adjective.
expensive **more** expensive modern **more** modern

Some adjectives are irregular.
good **better** bad **worse**

IMPERATIVES

+	−
Turn left.	Don't turn left.
Come out of the shop.	Don't come out of the shop.

PLURALS

REGULAR	WORDS WITH *Y*	IRREGULAR
one job	one company	one man
two jobs	two compan**ies**	two men
one car	one nationality	one person
two cars	two nationalit**ies**	two people

POSSESSIVES

1 Possessive adjectives

I	**my**	he	**his**	we	**our**
you	**your**	she	**her**	you	**your**
		it	**its**	they	**their**

2 Possessive *'s*

It is Margaret's company. = It is the company of Margaret.
It is Ronaldo's apartment. = It is the apartment of Ronaldo.

Note: Ronaldo's from Brazil. = Ronaldo **is** from Brazil.

PREPOSITIONS

across 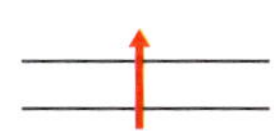

Go across the road.

at

1 at + place
Can we meet **at** the office?
2 at + time
Can we meet **at** four o'clock?

at the corner of 

It's **at the corner of** Fifteenth Street and Third Avenue.

between 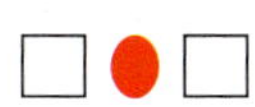

It's **between** the shop and the bank.

at the end of 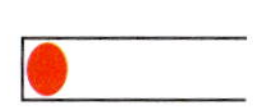

The lift is **at the end of** the corridor.

in

1 in 
She's **in** her car.
2 in + month
Can I see you **in** December?

into 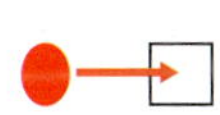

Go **into** the shop.

next to 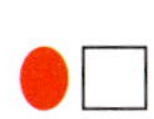

It's **next to** the restaurant.

on

1 on 
You walk **on** the pavement.

2 on + day
Can you meet me **on** Thursday?

out of

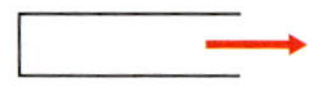

Come **out of** the office.

past

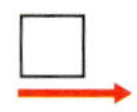

Go **past** the café.

round

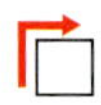

Go **round** the corner.

to

The train goes **to** Paris.

PRESENT SIMPLE

to work

+	−	?
I work	I don't work	Do I work?
You work	You don't work	Do you work?
He works	He doesn't work	Does he work?
She works	She doesn't work	Does she work?
It works	It doesn't work	Does it work?
We work	We don't work	Do we work?
You work	You don't work	Do you work?
They work	They don't work	Do they work?

to go

+	−	?
I go	I don't go	Do I go?
You go	You don't go	Do you go?
He goes	He doesn't go	Does he go?
She goes	She doesn't go	Does she go?
It goes	It doesn't go	Does it go?
We go	We don't go	Do we go?
You go	You don't go	Do you go?
They go	They don't go	Do they go?

to have

⊕	⊖	?
I have	I don't have	Do I have?
You have	You don't have	Do you have?
He has	He doesn't have	Does he have?
She has	She doesn't have	Does she have?
It has	It doesn't have	Does it have?
We have	We don't have	Do we have?
You have	You don't have	Do you have?
They have	They don't have	Do they have?

SHORT ANSWERS

to be

Are you from the USA?	Yes, I am.	No, I'm not.
Is she Maria?	Yes, she is.	No, she isn't.

can

Can you hear me?	Yes, I can.	No, I can't.
Can we meet at six?	Yes, we can.	No, we can't.

Present simple

Do you speak English?	Yes, I do.	No, I don't.
Does he drive a car?	Yes, he does.	No, he doesn't.

SOME AND *ANY*

1 Singular and plural

	SINGULAR	PLURAL
⊕	There is **a** hotel in the city.	There are **some** hotels in the city.
⊖	There isn't **a** hotel in the city.	There aren't **any** hotels in the city.
?	Is there **a** hotel in the city?	Are there **any** hotels in the city?

2 *some* or *any* in questions

You know the person has information:
Can I have **some** information, please?

You don't know if the person has information:
Do you have **any** information?

THERE IS AND *THERE ARE*

⊕

There is a computer in the office.
There are two computers in the office.
There are some computers in the office.

⊖

There isn't a computer in the office.
There aren't any computers in the office.

?

Is there a computer in the office?
Are there two computers in the office?
Are there any computers in the office?

TO BE

⊕	
I am	I'm
You are	You're
He is	He's
She is	She's
It is	It's
We are	We're
You are	You're
They are	They're

⊖		
I am not	–	(I'm not)
You are not	You aren't	(You're not)
He is not	He isn't	(He's not)
She is not	She isn't	(She's not)
It is not	It isn't	(It's not)
We are not	We aren't	(We're not)
You are not	You aren't	(You're not)
They are not	They aren't	(They're not)

?
Am I … ?
Are you … ?
Is he … ?
Is she … ?
Is it … ?
Are we … ?
Are you … ?
Are they … ?

WANT

1 *want* + noun

He wants a mobile phone.
He doesn't want a mobile phone.
Does he want a mobile phone?

2 *want to* + verb

He wants to leave.
He doesn't want to leave.
Does he want to leave?

transcripts

1 first words

page 4 exercise **2** (CD Track 1)

Hello. Goodbye. Thank you. Please.
Sorry. OK.

page 5 exercise **4** (CD Track 2)

WOMAN Hello.
MAN Hello.
WOMAN Yes?
MAN Coffee.
WOMAN Sorry?
MAN Coffee!
WOMAN Sorry?
MAN Coffee! Coffee!
WOMAN Sorry?
MAN Oh! Coffee, please.
WOMAN OK. Coffee.
MAN Thank you.
WOMAN One dollar.
MAN One dollar? One dollar?
WOMAN Oh, sorry. One dollar, *please.*
MAN OK.
WOMAN Thank you.
MAN Goodbye.
WOMAN Thank you. Goodbye.

page 6 exercise **2** (CD Track 3)

Hello. I'm Leo. And I'm Charles. Hello.
You're Tony. And you're Jacques.

page 6 exercise **3** (CD Track 4)

Hello. I'm Maria.
And I'm John. Hello.

page 6 exercise **4** (CD Track 5)

It's Wall Street.
He's Donald Trump.
She's Hillary Clinton.

page 7 exercise **6** (CD Track 6)

We're Jaguar.
They're Nissan.

page 7 exercise **9** (CD Track 7)

He's the Sultan of Brunei.
He's Karl Marx.
She's Demi Moore.
She's Aung Suu Kyi.
It's a dollar.
It's a Sony Walkman.
They're Venus and Serena Williams.
They're Big Macs.

page 8 exercise **1** (CD Track 8)

Can I have … ?
Can I have a coffee, please?

page 8 exercise **2/3** (CD Track 9)

WOMAN Sorry! Hello! Hello!
MAN Yes?
WOMAN Oh, hello, yes. Can I have the menu, please?
MAN The menu? Of course.
WOMAN Thank you.

WOMAN Hello. OK?
MAN Yes, OK, thank you. Can I have a coffee, please?
WOMAN A coffee, of course ... There you are.
MAN Thank you.

WOMAN Hello. Can I have a ticket to York, please?
MAN A ticket to York ... £10, please.
WOMAN Thank you.

WOMAN Hello.
MAN Hello. Can I have a map, please?
WOMAN A map?
MAN Yes. A map of the city.
WOMAN A map of the city. OK. This one?
MAN Yes. Yes, please. Can I have that one, please?
WOMAN Of course.

MAN Anything else?
WOMAN No, no thank you. Can I have the bill, please?
MAN The bill? Yes. Um … There you are.
WOMAN Thank you.
MAN Thank you.

WOMAN Yes?
MAN Hello. Can I have a timetable, please?
WOMAN A timetable. OK.
MAN Thank you. Goodbye.
WOMAN Bye.

page 9 exercise **6** (CD Track 10)

WOMAN Hello?
MAN Oh, hello, yes.
WOMAN So, dinner. Tomato soup or salad?
MAN Can I have tomato soup, please?
WOMAN Tomato soup. And then chicken and rice or pasta?
MAN Can I have pasta, please?
WOMAN Sorry?
MAN Can I have pasta, please?
WOMAN Pasta. And fruit or cheese?
MAN Can I have cheese, please?
WOMAN Cheese. Thank you.
MAN Thank you.

2 surviving

page 10 exercise **1** (CD Track 11)

zero one two three four five six

page 10 exercise **3** (CD Track 12)

Can I have three menus, please?
Can I have six coffees, please?
Can I have five tickets, please?
Can I have four maps, please?

page 10 exercise **4** (CD Track 13)

How much is it? It's two euros.
How much is it? It's six dollars.

page 10 exercise **6** (CD Track 14)

How much is it? It's one dollar.
How much is it? It's six euros.
How much is it? It's five dollars.
How much is it? It's four euros.
How much is it? It's three dollars.
How much is it? It's two euros.

page 11 exercise **8** (CD Track 15)

seven eight nine ten eleven twelve

page 11 exercise **9** (CD Track 16)

What time is it? It's nine o'clock.

page 11 exercise **10** (CD Track 17)

1 What time is it? It's eight o'clock.
2 What time is it? It's twelve o'clock.
3 What time is it? It's one o'clock.
4 What time is it? It's five o'clock.
5 What time is it? It's two o'clock.

page 12 exercise **2** (CD Track 18)

1 Is he Mike?
2 Are you OK?
3 Is she Leila?
4 Is it $5?
5 Are they sorry?

page 12 exercise **3** (CD Track 19)

Who are you?
How are you?

page 12 exercise **4** (CD Track 20)

1 JIM Hello. Are you André?
YOSHI No, I'm not. Sorry!
JIM Oh. Are you Stephan?
YOSHI No. No, I'm not.
JIM Oh. Who are you?
YOSHI I'm Yoshi.
JIM Ah, yes! Yoshi! Of course. Yoshi, I'm Jim … Jim Dakota.

2 CLAUDIA Clara? Hello, Clara.
CLARA Claudia! Hey, Claudia. Hello! How are you?
CLAUDIA Fine, thank you. How are you?
CLARA Fine. Fine, thank you.

page 12 exercise **7** (CD Track 21)

1 How much is it?
2 Who are they?
3 How is he?
4 Are you Stan?
5 What time is it?
6 Is she Maria?

page 13 exercise **8** (CD Track 22)

Are you Anna?	Yes, I am.
Are you Anna?	No, I'm not.
Is it ten euros?	Yes, it is.
Is it ten euros?	No, it isn't.

page 13 exercise **10** (CD Track 23)

1 Is he Ronald Reagan?
No, he isn't. He's John F. Kennedy.
2 Is she Gwyneth Paltrow?
Yes, she is.
3 Is she Anna Kournikova?
Yes, she is.
4 Is he George Michael?
No, he isn't. He's Elton John.
5 Is it the Eiffel Tower?
Yes, it is.
6 Are they The Spice Girls?
No, they're not. They're The Beatles.

page 14 exercise **1** (CD Track 24)

WOMAN Hello.
MAN Oh, hello. Can I have six timetables, please?
WOMAN Sorry. Can you say that again, please?
MAN Oh! Can I have six timetables, please?
WOMAN Sorry. Can you speak more slowly, please?
MAN Can – I – have – six – timetables – please?
WOMAN No. I'm sorry. I don't understand.
MAN Six timetables, please! Six timetables!

page 14 exercise **2** (CD Track 25)

I'm sorry. I don't understand.
Can you say that again, please?
Can you speak more slowly, please?

page 14 exercise **4/5** (CD Track 26)

MAN 1 What time is it?
MAN 2 Can you say that again, please?
MAN 1 What time is it?
MAN 2 Can you speak more slowly, please?
MAN 1 What – time – is – it?
MAN 2 Oh! Five o'clock.
MAN 1 Sorry?
MAN 2 Five o'clock.
MAN 1 Thank you.

page 15 exercise **7** (CD Track 27)

MAN 1 Hello. Can I have a map, please?
MAN 2 I'm sorry. I don't understand.
MAN 1 A map. Can I have a map, please?
MAN 2 Oh, a map. Yes. Of course.
MAN 1 How much is it?
MAN 2 I'm sorry. Can you say that again?
MAN 1 How much is it?
MAN 2 It's $12.10, please.
MAN 1 Can you speak more slowly, please?
MAN 2 I'm sorry. $12.10, please.
MAN 1 $12.10. Thank you.
MAN 2 Thank you. Goodbye.

review 1

page 17 exercise **4** (CD Track 28)

coffee ticket again tomato eleven understand

page 17 exercise **5** (CD Track 28)

MAN 1 Hello.
WOMAN 1 Hi.

WOMAN 2 Hello.
MAN 2 Good morning.

MAN 1 Hello.
MAN 2 Good afternoon.

WOMAN 1 Hello.
WOMAN 2 Good evening.

MAN 2 Goodbye.
WOMAN 1 See you.

MAN 1 Good night.
WOMAN 2 Good night.

page 17 exercise **6** (CD Track 28)

Hello. Hi. Good morning.
Good afternoon. Good evening.

Goodbye. See you. Good night.

3 people

page 18 exercise **1** (CD Track 29)

name job company country

page 18 exercise **2** (CD Track 30)

MAN What's your name?
NETZER My name's Boris Netzer.
MAN Where are you from?
NETZER I'm from Germany.
MAN What's the name of your company?
NETZER It's City Consulting.
MAN What's your job?
NETZER I'm a businessman.

page 18 exercise **3** (CD Track 31)

MAN What's your name?
NETZER My name's Boris Netzer.

page 18 exercise **5** (CD Track 32)

1 a businessman
2 a teacher
3 a businesswoman
4 a student

page 19 exercise **7** (CD Track 33)

Italy France the UK Japan Germany
Russia the USA Canada

page 19 exercise **9** (CD Track 34)

What's your name?
What's your job?
What's the name of your company?
Where are you from?

page 19 exercise **10** (CD Track 35)

On the phone

MAN Hello. PP.com.
WOMAN Oh, hello. Patrick Partridge, please.
MAN Yes, of course. What's your name?
WOMAN My name's Jane Fong.

MAN What's the name of your company?
WOMAN It's City Consulting.
MAN Just a moment, please.

At a party

MAN I'm sorry. Are you from City Consulting?
WOMAN No, I'm not.
MAN Oh. What's the name of your company?
WOMAN I'm not from a company. I'm a student.
MAN Where are you from?
WOMAN I'm from the USA.
MAN The USA? Really?

page 20 exercise **1** (CD Track 36)

His name's George Soros. He's a businessman from Hungary. The name of his company is Quantum Fund.

page 20 exercise **3** (CD Track 37)

What's his name?	His name's George Soros.
What's his job?	He's a businessman.
Where's he from?	He's from Hungary.
What's the name of his company?	Its name is Quantum Fund.

page 20 exercise **4** (CD Track 38)

What's her name?	Her name's Carly Fiorina.
What's her job?	She's a businesswoman.
Where's she from?	She's from the USA.
What's the name of her company?	Its name's Hewlett-Packard.

page 21 exercise **8** (CD Track 39)

one person	two people
one job	two jobs
job	jobs
one name	two names
name	names
one company	two companies
company	companies
one man	two men
man	men
one woman	two women
woman	women

page 21 exercise **11** (CD Track 40)

1 What are their names?
Their names are Dave Filo and Jerry Yang.
2 What are their jobs?
They're businessmen.
3 Where are they from?
They're from California.
4 What's the name of their company?
Its name is Yahoo!

page 22 exercise **1** (CD Track 41)

Can I speak to John, please?
It's Groucho here.
Just a moment, please.

page 22 exercise **2** (CD Track 42)

WOMAN 1 Hello. City Consulting.
WOMAN 2 Hello. It's Luisa Briggs here. Can I speak to Tom Rogers, please?
WOMAN 1 Tom Rogers? Of course. What's the name of your company?
WOMAN 2 I'm from PA.com.
WOMAN 1 Can you say that again, please?
WOMAN 2 I'm from PA.com.
WOMAN 1 Thank you. Just a moment, please.

page 23 exercise **6** (CD Track 43)

A1 Hello. A1 Taxis.
DAVID Oh, hello.
A1 Just a moment, please. Yes. Hello.
DAVID Hello. Can I have a taxi, please?
A1 Sure. What's your name?
DAVID David Norman.
A1 David Norman. Where are you?
DAVID I'm at the airport.
A1 Can you speak more slowly, please?
DAVID Yes. I'm – at – the – airport.
A1 At the airport. Fine. Five minutes, OK?
DAVID Yes. Thank you. Goodbye.

4 arrangements

page 24 exercise **1** (CD Track 44)

meet come go see send call

page 24 exercise **3** (CD Track 45)

Doris,
Can we meet at three o'clock on Monday? You can come to my hotel or I can go to your office. Please call on 010 4456 1123 or send an e-mail.
See you on Monday!
Bruce

page 24 exercise **4** (CD Track 46)

Monday Tuesday Wednesday Thursday
Friday Saturday Sunday

page 25 exercise **7** (CD Track 47)

You live in an apartment.
You stay in a hotel.
You work in an office.
You eat in a restaurant.
You shop in a shop.

page 25 exercise **8** (CD Track 48)

come to	Can you come to my apartment?
go to	Can we go to your office?
meet at	Can we meet at your shop?
at	Can we meet at 5 o'clock?
on	Can we meet on Thursday?

page 26 exercise **2** (CD Track 49)

Can I speak to Maria, please?
Can they come to my office on Monday?
Can you say that again?
Can you speak more slowly, please?
Can I have a coffee, please?
Can we meet at the restaurant?

page 26 exercise **3** (CD Track 50)

With this mobile phone, you can call people and you can send e-mails.

With this phone, you can call people, but you can't send e-mails.

With this computer, you can't call people, but you can send e-mails.

page 27 exercise **6/7** (CD Track 51)

MAN Hello. Can I speak to Maggie Khan, please?
WOMAN No, I'm sorry, you can't. She's in a meeting. Can I help you? I'm Maggie's secretary.
MAN Oh, yes. It's Nasser Hutchins here.
WOMAN Nasser Hutchins. Which company are you from?
MAN I'm from the BB Bank.
WOMAN I'm sorry. Can you say that again?
MAN Sorry, yes. I'm from the BB Bank. Can Maggie meet me in London on Tuesday?
WOMAN No, I'm sorry, she can't. She's in New York on Tuesday.
MAN Oh. Can she meet me on Monday?
WOMAN Monday? Yes, she can. Can you come to her office at one o'clock?
MAN Yes, I can. One o'clock. Thank you.
WOMAN Thank you. Goodbye.

page 28 exercise **4** (CD Track 52)

MAN When is Jill's plane?
WOMAN It's at 12 o'clock on Wednesday.
MAN Can Clara meet Jill on Wednesday?
WOMAN No, she can't.
MAN When can she meet Jill?
WOMAN On Thursday.
MAN How can they speak when Clara isn't in the office?
WOMAN Jill can call her mobile phone.

review 2

page 31 exercise **6** (CD Track 53)

eight two where what who
Wednesday

page 31 exercise **7** (CD Track 53)

her here

page 31 exercise **8** (CD Track 53)

mobile phone name plane before
office come rice nine have

page 31 exercise **9** (CD Track 53)

A B C D
bad B – A – D
cab C – A – B

E F G H
face F – A – C – E
hedge H – E – D – G – E

I J K L
Jack J – A – C – K
bill B – I – L – L

M N O P
phone P – H – O – N – E
mail M – A – I – L

Q R S T U
quiet Q – U – I – E – T
trust T – R – U – S – T
restaurant R – E – S – T – A – U – R – A – N – T

V W X Y Z
wave W – A – V – E
why W – H – Y
X-ray X – R – A – Y
zero Z – E – R – O

5 travel

page 32 exercise **1** (CD Track 54)

station check-in boarding gate airport
ticket office platform

page 32 exercise **3** (CD Track 55)

thirteen fourteen fifteen sixteen
seventeen eighteen nineteen twenty
twenty-one twenty-two twenty-three
twenty-four twenty-five twenty-six
twenty-seven twenty-eight twenty-nine

page 33 exercise **5** (CD Track 56)

thirty forty fifty sixty seventy eighty
ninety a hundred

page 33 exercise **8** (CD Track 57)

1 The 15:30 train to Minsk is now at platform 17.
The 15:42 train to Budapest leaves from platform 14.
The 16:10 train to Warsaw leaves from platform 12.
The 16:15 express to Vienna leaves from platform 19.

2 The 20:15 plane to Atlanta is now boarding at gate 42.
For the 20:40 plane to Dallas, please go to gate 51.
For the 21:10 plane to Montreal, go to gate 16.
The 21:25 plane to Bogotá will board through gate 33.

page 34 exercise **1** (CD Track 58)

My name's Sasha Amado. I'm a businesswoman from Brazil. I live in Santos and I work in São Paulo. I have a VW and I go to work by car.

page 36 exercise **1** (CD Track 59)

Can I have some information … ?
Can I have some information about the plane to Seoul, please?
What time does it leave?
What time does it arrive?

page 36 exercise **2** (CD Track 60)

MAN Hello. Travel enquiries.
WOMAN Hello. Can I have some information about the plane to Seoul on Friday evening?
MAN Sure.
WOMAN What time does it leave?
MAN It leaves at 19:40.
WOMAN And what time does it arrive?
MAN It arrives at Kimpo International Airport in Seoul at 6:30 on Saturday.
WOMAN 6:30 on Saturday. Thank you. Goodbye.
MAN Thank you. Goodbye.

page 37 exercise **6** (CD Track 61)

1 MAN Can I check in for the plane to Bangkok?
WOMAN Yes, of course.
MAN Thank you. What time does the plane leave?
WOMAN It leaves at 22:15. Can I have your ticket, please?
MAN Yes. Here you are. And which boarding gate is it from?
WOMAN It goes from gate 72.
MAN 72.
WOMAN Can I see your passport, please?
MAN Yes, of course. So, what time does it arrive in Bangkok?
WOMAN It arrives at 18:40. Local time.
MAN 18:40. Thank you.

2 MAN Yes?
WOMAN Hello. Can I have a ticket to Turin, please?
MAN Yes, of course.
WOMAN How much is it?
MAN It's €98.
WOMAN What time does it leave?
MAN It leaves at 14:44.
WOMAN I'm sorry, can you say that again?
MAN 14:44.
WOMAN 14:44. And what time does it arrive?
MAN It arrives at 17:57.
WOMAN Thank you. Which platform is it?
MAN Platform 12.
WOMAN Thank you.
MAN Thank you. Goodbye.

6 work

page 38 exercise **1** (CD Track 62)

1 a factory worker
2 a boss a secretary
3 a salesperson a customer

page 38 exercise **2** (CD Track 63)

INTERVIEWER Hello.
SECRETARY Oh, hello.
INTERVIEWER What do you do?
SECRETARY I'm a secretary. You know, I help people in the office.
INTERVIEWER You help people.
SECRETARY Yes. I answer the phone, I send e-mails. That kind of thing.
INTERVIEWER Thank you.

INTERVIEWER I'm sorry! I'm sorry! What do you do?
BOSS I'm a boss.
INTERVIEWER A boss?
BOSS Yes, a boss. I manage people, I manage lots of people, and I'm very, very busy. Now, excuse me!
INTERVIEWER Oh, I'm sorry. Yes, of course.

INTERVIEWER Hello. What do you do?
WORKER Sorry. Can you say that again?
INTERVIEWER What do you do?

WORKER I'm a factory worker.
INTERVIEWER A factory worker.
WORKER Yes. I make things. We make cars here.
INTERVIEWER Yes. Yes. Thank you.

INTERVIEWER I'm sorry. What do you do?
SALESPERSON What?
INTERVIEWER What do you do? What's your job?
SALESPERSON I'm a salesperson. I sell things.
INTERVIEWER You sell things.
SALESPERSON Yes. I sell things … and I drive a car.
INTERVIEWER Sorry … Bye!

INTERVIEWER Hello.
CUSTOMER Oh, hello.
INTERVIEWER What do you do?
CUSTOMER I'm sorry, can you speak more slowly?
INTERVIEWER What do you do? What's your job?
CUSTOMER Oh, I don't have a job. I don't work. I'm a customer.
INTERVIEWER Ah! A customer.
CUSTOMER Yes. I buy things.
INTERVIEWER I can see that!

page 39 exercise **5** (CD Track 64)

Who does he work for?
He works for BP.
Who does she work for?
She works for Compaq.
Who do they work for?
They work for Vodafone.

page 39 exercise **7** (CD Track 65)

a manufacturing company
a supermarket
a charity

page 40 exercise **1** (CD Track 66)

I don't work for a company because I don't have a job.
She doesn't understand computers so she doesn't send e-mails.

page 40 exercise **3** (CD Track 67)

1 He's a customer. He doesn't sell things, he buys things.
2 We're factory workers. We don't work for a supermarket, we work for a manufacturing company.
3 I'm a salesperson. I don't manage people, I sell things.
4 It's a charity. It doesn't make things, it helps people.

page 41 exercise **4** (CD Track 68)

Do you speak English?	Yes, I do.
Do you speak English?	No, I don't.
Does she understand?	Yes, she does.
Does she understand?	No, she doesn't.

page 42 exercise **2** (CD Track 69)

MAN 1 This is Yeping Wang.
MAN 2 And this is Hillary.
WOMAN 1 Pleased to meet you.
WOMAN 2 And you.

page 42 exercise **4** (CD Track 70)

WOMAN Hello. Hello, Peter. Now Anna, this is Peter and, Peter, this is Anna.
ANNA Pleased to meet you.
PETER And you.
WOMAN Peter is a salesperson for Silverchip.
PETER That's right.
ANNA Silverchip. What kind of company is it?
PETER It's a manufacturing company. Yes. A manufacturing company. It makes mobile phones.
ANNA Mobile phones. Oh.
PETER And who do you work for, Anna?
ANNA I work for AJ.com.
PETER Ah, I know! Do you sell computers?
ANNA No, we don't.
PETER Oh. So, what do you sell?
ANNA We sell plane tickets.
PETER Plane tickets. Right. So are you a salesperson?
ANNA No. No, I'm not.

PETER What do you do?
ANNA Well, it's my company. I'm the boss.
PETER Ooh. The boss, eh?

review 3

page 44 exercise **4** (CD Track 71)

13 30 14 40 15 16 17 50 60 70
80 18 90 19

page 45 exercise **10** (CD Track 71)

twenty past six	five to eleven
five fifteen	ten past nine
quarter to one	quarter past seven
twenty-five to three	six forty-five
half past eight	twelve o'clock

7 products

page 46 exercise **4** (CD Track 72)

bad	good
expensive	cheap
slow	fast
modern	old
ugly	beautiful
big	small

page 47 exercise **5** (CD Track 73)

DJ And now time for a break …
MAN Computer Hut is the number one shop for business computers. Do you work for a big company? Then come to Computer Hut. We have big, fast computers for the modern office. Do you travel for business? Then come to Computer Hut. We have small computers for the train, car and plane. Oh … and we're not expensive.
SONG Computers for your business, in the office, train and plane. Computers are our business. Computer Hut's our name.
WOMAN Hi. I'm a modern woman and I like modern clothes. So I buy my clothes at Sasha Noir. I like Sasha Noir's clothes because they're beautiful. And also … Shhhh! I like them because they're cheap.
MAN Sasha Noir. Beautiful clothes for modern women. Shhhh!

page 51 exercise **3** (CD Track 74)

WOMAN Good morning, sir. Can I help you?
MAN Yes. I want to buy a suit.
WOMAN What kind of suit do you want?
MAN I want a good, modern business suit.
WOMAN How about this one, sir? Do you like this one?
MAN Oh, yes. Yes, I do. How much is it?
WOMAN $990, sir.
MAN Oh. It's very expensive. Do you have a cheaper one?
WOMAN Oh, yes, sir. We have a good suit for $199.
MAN Can I try it on?
WOMAN Of course, sir … So, how is it, sir?
MAN Well, it's very small. Do you have a bigger one?
WOMAN No, I'm sorry, sir, we don't.
MAN But it is very, very cheap. I want it. Can I have it, please?

8 bookings

page 52 exercise **2** (CD Track 75)

1 double	*4* bath	*7* gym
2 shower	*5* bar	*8* room
3 swimming	*6* single	

page 52 exercise **3** (CD Track 76)

RECEPTIONIST Good afternoon. Can I help you?
CUSTOMER Hello. Yes. I want to book a room, please.
RECEPTIONIST Yes, of course. What kind of room do you want?
CUSTOMER Well, it's for two people, so a double room, please.
RECEPTIONIST A double room. With a bath or with a shower?
CUSTOMER A double room with a bath, please.
RECEPTIONIST A double room with a bath. And when do you want it?
CUSTOMER From the first of April to the sixth of April, please.
RECEPTIONIST Well, from today, the first of April to the sixth of April. Yes, that's OK.
CUSTOMER And how much is it?
RECEPTIONIST It's $200 a night.
CUSTOMER $200 a night. Hmm. That's expensive. Can I have some information about the hotel?
RECEPTIONIST Of course.
CUSTOMER Is there a restaurant?
RECEPTIONIST No, I'm sorry. This is a small hotel, so there isn't a restaurant, but there's a bar and there's room service.
CUSTOMER A bar and room service.
RECEPTIONIST There's a small swimming pool, too.
CUSTOMER Good. OK. Can I book it?
RECEPTIONIST Yes, of course. What's your name?

page 53 exercise **5** (CD Track 77)

January February March April May
June July August September October
November December

page 53 exercise **8** (CD Track 78)

RECEPTIONIST Hello. PH car rental. Can I help you?
MAN Hello. Yes. I want to rent a car.
RECEPTIONIST Of course. What kind of car do you want?
MAN Oooh, a fast one. A small, fast car.
RECEPTIONIST A small, fast car. Yes. And when do you want it?
MAN From the twenty-sixth of May to the seventh of June, please.
RECEPTIONIST From the twenty-sixth of May to the seventh of June. Just a moment, please. Yes, that's no problem.
MAN How much is it?
RECEPTIONIST Well, we have one for $175 a day.
MAN $175 a day! $175 a day! That's too expensive! Do you have a cheaper one?
RECEPTIONIST Er … just a moment, please. No, I'm sorry, we don't.
MAN Oh. $175 a day? Oh, OK, I'll take it.

page 55 exercise **3** (CD Track 79)

RECEPTIONIST Good evening. The Ritz Hotel.
CUSTOMER Good evening. Can I book a room, please?
RECEPTIONIST Yes, of course.
CUSTOMER Are there any double rooms with a bath?
RECEPTIONIST No, but there are some double rooms with a shower.
CUSTOMER And are there any single rooms with a bath?
RECEPTIONIST No, I'm sorry, there aren't. But, of course, there are some single rooms with a shower.
CUSTOMER Good. Is there a restaurant?
RECEPTIONIST No, there isn't, but there is a bar.
CUSTOMER And is there a swimming pool?

RECEPTIONIST Yes, there is.
CUSTOMER Thank you.

page 56 exercise **2** (CD Track 80)

1 BOSS Robert?
SECRETARY Yes.
BOSS Can you book a flight from New York to Paris for me?
SECRETARY A flight from New York to Paris.
BOSS Yes.
SECRETARY When do you want to go?
BOSS The twenty-second of April.
SECRETARY The twenty-second of April.
BOSS Yes.
SECRETARY And when do you want to return?
BOSS I want to return on the first of May.
SECRETARY So, leaving on the twenty-second of April, returning on the first of May. OK. Oh, yes, what class do you want?
BOSS What class? Business class, of course.
SECRETARY Business class. OK.

2 AGENT Hello, PH Travel.
CALLER Hello. Can I book a hotel room in Paris, please?
AGENT Is that Paris, France?
CALLER Yes, of course it is.
AGENT Good. A hotel room in Paris, France. And when do you want it?
CALLER From the nineteenth of December to the twenty-third of December.
AGENT From the nineteenth to the twenty-third of December. Right. And what kind of room do you want?
CALLER Oh, it's just for me, so can I have a single room, please?
AGENT A single room. With a bath or with a shower?
CALLER A single room with a shower, please.
AGENT A single room with a shower. Good. Well, there are lots of hotels in Paris, France, but in December … Hmm.

review 4

page 59 exercise **4** (CD Track 81)

bar	bath
modern	company
want	bad
please	meeting
good	food
web	better
go	old
click	big
but	June
suit	you

page 59 exercise **5** (CD Track 81)

one thousand
two thousand
one hundred thousand
one million
one thousand and forty
two thousand and seven
thirty thousand four hundred and sixty-five
four hundred and six thousand five hundred and twelve
one million and fifty-nine

page 59 exercise **7** (CD Track 81)

forty-two thousand
one hundred and fifty thousand
six thousand four hundred
one million
nine thousand nine hundred and ninety-nine
twelve thousand six hundred and sixty-six
five hundred thousand five hundred and twenty
seventeen thousand one hundred and seventy-seven

page 59 exercise **9** (CD Track 81)

the twelfth of May two thousand and four
the eleventh of November two thousand and nine
October the twenty-sixth two thousand and eighteen
the thirty-first of August two thousand and twenty-five

the third of January two thousand and nineteen
the nineteenth of September two thousand and eight

9 directions

page 60 exercise **3** (CD Track 82)

British English	**US English**
corridor	corridor – it's the same word
lift	elevator
ground floor	first floor
toilets	restrooms
pavement	sidewalk
cashpoint	ATM
underground station	subway station

page 61 exercise **5** (CD Track 83)

1 MAN Excuse me.
WOMAN Yes. Can I help you?
MAN Er … where are the restrooms?
WOMAN I'm sorry, can you say that again?
MAN Um … Where are the restrooms?
WOMAN Restrooms? … Ah! You mean the toilets! They're at the end of the corridor!
MAN At the end of the corridor.
WOMAN Yes, just there!
MAN Thank you. Thank you.

2 MAN Hello. Can I help you?
WOMAN Yes. Excuse me. Where is the restaurant in this hotel?
MAN Ah. Take the lift to the first floor.
WOMAN I'm sorry. I don't understand.
MAN The restaurant. It's on the first floor. So, take the lift …
WOMAN You mean 'elevator'. Not lift, elevator.
MAN Yes. Yes, of course. Elevator. Take the elevator to the first floor.
WOMAN But we're on the first floor now.
MAN No, no. This is the ground floor.
WOMAN Ha! You British! You mean take the elevator to the second floor, right?
MAN Yes, I'm sorry. Of course. Take the elevator to the second floor.
WOMAN Good. OK. So – where – is – the elevator?
MAN Ah! It's … it's next to the bar.
WOMAN Next to the bar … Oh, I see. Thank you.
MAN Yes. Thank you.

3 POLICEMAN Hey! Hey! Hey, you!
WOMAN Yes, officer. Can I help you?
POLICEMAN You can't leave your car here.
WOMAN I'm sorry. What's the problem?
POLICEMAN It's on the sidewalk! You can't park your car on the sidewalk!
WOMAN You mean the pavement? Oh, I am sorry. Just a moment, please.

page 62 exercise **2** (CD Track 84)

RECEPTIONIST So room 201. Here's the key.
GUEST Thank you. How do I get there?
RECEPTIONIST OK. Take the lift to the second floor. Then come out of the lift, turn right and go straight down the corridor. Room 201 is at the end of the corridor. It's the seventh door on the left.
GUEST So, take the lift to the second floor. Come out of the lift, turn right. Go straight down the corridor, and it's the seventh door on the left.
RECEPTIONIST That's right.
GUEST Thank you.

page 64 exercise **1** (CD Track 85)

WOMAN Excuse me.
MAN Yes?
WOMAN I'm lost. Where's Fifth Avenue?
MAN Fifth Avenue?
WOMAN Yes, is it near here?
MAN Yes, it is.
WOMAN Oh, good. How do I get there?

MAN I'm afraid I can't help you.
WOMAN I'm sorry. What do you mean?
MAN Well, you're in Fifth Avenue.
WOMAN You mean, this is Fifth Avenue?
MAN Yes, of course it is. Look at the sign.
WOMAN Fifth Avenue! Thank you! Now, where are the shops?

page 64 exercise **3** (CD Track 86)

1 Go out of the Waldorf Astoria and turn right. Go across the road and take the first on your left, that's East 51st Street. Go straight down East 51st Street, across Madison Avenue and at the corner of Fifth Avenue, turn right and then go straight down the road. Go past the Olympic Tower and the subway station is on the corner of the second street on the right.

2 Go out of Saks Fifth Avenue and turn right. Go straight down Fifth Avenue. Go past the Olympic Tower and the subway station and then turn right down East 55th Street. Hmmm. It's the sixth on the right. Then, go down East 55th Street and the Sony Building is the first on your left, just round the corner.

10 problems

page 66 exercise **3** (CD Track 87)

1 CLERK Good morning.
PASSENGER Good morning. Can I check in for the flight to Delhi, please?
CLERK The flight to Delhi?
PASSENGER Yes, I'm sorry. I know I'm late.
CLERK Don't worry. Here's your boarding pass. Go straight to the boarding gate.
PASSENGER Thank you.

2 PASSENGER Excuse me. Can I have some information about the flight to Sydney, please? BA 43210.
CLERK BA 43210. Oh … I'm afraid it's cancelled.
PASSENGER Well, when's the next flight?
CLERK Tomorrow morning at 6:00.
PASSENGER Tomorrow morning!
CLERK Yes, I'm sorry. Do you want to wait in the lounge?
PASSENGER What? Wait in the lounge!

page 67 exercise **6** (CD Track 88)

GUEST Hello.
RECEPTIONIST Good morning.
GUEST Can I check out, please?
RECEPTIONIST Yes, of course. What's your room number?
GUEST Er … 314.
RECEPTIONIST 314 … Mrs Blake. Just one night.
GUEST Yes.
RECEPTIONIST How do you want to pay?
GUEST Can I pay by credit card?
RECEPTIONIST Yes, of course … Thank you … Oh. I'm sorry. Hmm. There's a problem with our machine.
GUEST Oh. Um … Can I write a cheque?
RECEPTIONIST Yes, of course.
GUEST Do you have a pen?
RECEPTIONIST Yes. Here you are.

page 68 exercise **3** (CD Track 89)

ANNA Hi, Carl. What's the problem?
CARL Hi. I'm late for the meeting.
ANNA When does it start?
CARL Nine thirty.
ANNA Nine thirty? It's nine thirty now! Who's the meeting with?
CARL It's with my boss and her boss! Now, where's meeting room two?
ANNA It's on the second floor at the end of the corridor.
CARL Which floor?
ANNA The second floor!

page 69 exercise **4/5** (CD Track 90)

TOM Major Tom to Ground Control. Major Tom to Ground Control.
CONTROL Major Tom? This is Ground Control. What's the situation, Tom?
TOM It's a bad situation, Ground Control.
CONTROL How bad is it, Tom? How bad is it?
TOM It's very bad, Ground Control. There's a big problem here.
CONTROL How big is the problem, Tom?
TOM Well, we have a dead circuit on the QVCA17TF here.
CONTROL Sorry, Tom, can you say that again, please?
TOM There's a problem with ... Oh, don't worry, Ground Control. It's a very big problem, OK?
CONTROL OK. What can you do about it, Tom? What can you do?
TOM Don't worry, Ground Control. I can do something. I'm good at my job.
CONTROL We know you're good, Tom. But how good are you?
TOM Oh, I'm good. I'm very good. I'm …
CONTROL Major Tom? Can you hear me, Major Tom? Can you hear me, Major Tom?

page 70 exercise **1** (CD Track 91)

ANSWERPHONE This is the answerphone for Ravi Shipman. I'm afraid I can't take your call at the moment, so please leave a message after the tone or ring my mobile on 07771 456321.

KATIE Hello, Ravi … Ravi, are you there? … Um … OK. It's Katie here and it's half past nine, yes 9:30 on Tuesday. Yes, I know. I'm sorry, I'm late for the meeting. But … well, I'm at the airport. My plane's delayed … So, if you have any questions, please call me on my mobile – the number's 07861 424248, that's 07861 424248 – and, of course, please start the meeting without me. Bye.

page 70 exercise **2** (CD Track 92)

This is the answerphone for Ravi Shipman. I'm afraid I can't take your call at the moment, so please leave a message after the tone or ring my mobile on 07771 456321.

page 70 exercise **3** (CD Track 93)

This is the voicemail for Ravi Shipman. I'm sorry I can't answer your call at the moment, so please speak after the bleep or call my office on 0787 56522.

review 5

page 72 exercise **2** (CD Track 94)

as answer business solve days weeks
message phrase excuse me outside

wordlists

1 first words

a ....

am ....

and ....

are ....

bill ....

can ....

cheese ....

chicken ....

coffee ....

dollar ....

fruit ....

goodbye ....

have ....

he ....

hello ....

I ....

is ....

it ....

map ....

menu ....

no ....

of course ....

OK ....

pasta ....

please ....

rice ....

salad ....

she ....

sorry ....

thank you ....

the ....

they ....

ticket ....

timetable ....

tomato soup ....

we ....

yes ....

you ....

2 surviving

again ....

don't ....

eight ....

eleven ....

euros ....

fine ....

five ....

four ....

how ....

how much ....

more ....

nine ....

not ....

o'clock ....

one ....

say ....

seven ....

six ....

slowly ....

speak ....

ten ....

that ....
three ....
twelve ....
two ....
understand ....
what time ....
who ....
zero ....

3 people

airport ....
businessman ....
businesswoman ....
Canada ....
company ....
country ....
France ....
from ....
Germany ....
her ....
here ....
his ....
Internet ....
Italy ....
its ....
Japan ....
job ....
just ....
man ....
men ....
moment ....
my ....
name ....
our ....
people ....
person ....
Russia ....
student ....
taxi ....
teacher ....
their ....
UK ....
USA ....
where ....
woman ....
women ....
your ....

4 arrangements

after ....
an ....
apartment ....
at ....
before ....
Best wishes ....
call ....
can't ....
come ....
computer ....
Dear ....
diary ....
eat ....
e-mail ....
Friday ....
go ....
help ....
Hi ....
hotel ....
how about ....
in ....
live ....
meet ....
meeting ....
mobile phone ....
Monday ....
office ....

on ....
phone ....
plane ....
PS ....
Regards ....
restaurant ....
Saturday ....
secretary ....
see ....
send ....
shop ....
stay ....
Sunday ....
Thursday ....
to ....
Tuesday ....
Wednesday ....
which ....
work ....

5 travel

about ....
arrive ....
boarding gate ....
bus ....
by ....
check-in ....
do ....
drive ....
eighteen ....
eighty ....
enquiries ....
fifteen ....
fifty ....
fly ....
forty ....
fourteen ....
hundred ....
information ....
leave ....
local time ....
nineteen ....
ninety ....
on foot ....
passport ....
platform ....
seventeen ....
seventy ....
sixteen ....
sixty ....
some ....
station ....
thirteen ....
thirty ....
ticket office ....
train ....
travel ....
twenty ....

6 work

boss ....
buy ....
charity ....
customer ....
drink ....
factory ....
kind of ....
know ....
make ....
manage ....
manufacturing ....
salesperson ....
sell ....
smoke ....
supermarket ....
things ....

this ....
walk ....
worker ....

7 products

also ....
bad ....
beautiful ....
because ....
better ....
big ....
cheap ....
clothes ....
expensive ....
fast ....
food ....
good ....
hundreds ....
like ....
make (money) ....
modern ....
more ....
old ....
painting ....
slow ....
small ....
suit ....
that ....
ugly ....
very ....
want ....
worse ....

8 bookings

access ....
accommodation ....
any ....
April ....
August ....
bar ....
bath ....
beach ....
booking ....
car park ....
click ....
December ....
double room ....
February ....
first ....
flight ....
fourth ....
holiday ....
home ....
January ....
July ....
June ....
March ....
May ....
meal ....
November ....
October ....
rent ....
return ....
room service ....
search ....
second ....
September ....
shower ....
single room ....
snack ....
swimming pool ....
third ....
travel agent ....
trip ....
web page ....

9 directions

across ....
afraid ....
at the corner of ....
at the end of ....
ATM ....
between ....
cashpoint ....
corridor ....
directions ....
elevator ....
excuse me ....
first floor ....
ground floor ....
inside ....
into ....
left ....
lift ....
lost ....
mean ....
money ....
next to ....
out of ....
outside ....
past ....
pavement ....
restrooms ....
right ....
round ....
sidewalk ....
sign ....
straight down ....
subway station ....
take ....
toilets ....
turn ....
underground station ....

10 problems

answer ....
answerphone ....
as soon as possible ....
boarding ....
boarding pass ....
bleep ....
cancelled ....
cash ....
cheque ....
control ....
credit card ....
currency ....
delayed ....
destination ....
early ....
enough ....
late ....
leave (a message) ....
lounge ....
machine ....
message ....
next ....
pay ....
problem ....
ring ....
situation ....
solve ....
tone ....
voicemail ....
wait ....
without ....
write ....